REVOLT IN JUDEA:
THE ROAD TO MASADA

REVOLT IN JUDEA: THE ROAD TO MASADA

The eyewitness account by Flavius Josephus of the Roman campaign against Judea, the destruction of the Second Temple, and the heroism of Masada

Condensed and adapted for modern readers by
ALFRED H. TAMARIN

GALAHAD BOOKS · NEW YORK

To my wife . . .

Grateful acknowledgment is made to Harvard University Press and The Loeb Classical Library for permission to reprint from JOSEPHUS' THE JEWISH WAR, Books 1-7, translated by H. St. J. Thackeray.
Copyright © 1968 by Alfred H. Tamarin.
All rights reserved.
Library of Congress Catalog Card Number: 74-77010
ISBN 0-88365-283-8
Published by arrangement with Four Winds Press,
A Division of Scholastic Magazines, Inc.
Printed in the United States of America.
Jacket photo: Coin of Vespasian. Fototeca Unione

PREFACE	7
INTRODUCTION	9
CHRONOLOGY	31
I	33
II	53
III	69
IV	87
V	137
INDEX	155

PREFACE

Recent dramatic archaeological discoveries at Masada arrested the attention of the modern world. For two years (1963–1965), a team of archaeologists led by Professor Yigael Yadin of the Hebrew University excavated at this almost inaccessible mountain fortress overlooking the Dead Sea. On top of the mountain, the archaeologists found Jewish arrowheads and Roman stone missiles, charred timbers and the skeletal remains of a warrior, a woman, and a child lying close together. At the foot of the mountain, they found remnants of a Roman encampment.

The excavations revealed evidence that a tragic story told nineteen hundred years ago had actually happened. The Jewish-Roman historian Flavius Josephus, who lived in the first century A.D., had written about a band of Zealots who in 73 A.D. were the last to hold out against Rome. At Masada, these 960 men, women, and children committed mass suicide rather than fall into the hands of the Romans. The archaeologists found pottery sherds which may have been remnants of a lottery that decided who would be the last to die. Remains of a three-tiered structure verified Josephus' description of Herod's palace built on Masada in the first century B.C.

These discoveries at Masada revived popular interest in Josephus, who has always been considered a source of enormous value by the professional historian. In the minds of many of his co-religionists, the Jews, however, he has been more often regarded as a turncoat, if not a traitor.

Josephus was born Joseph ben Matthias, the son of a priestly Jewish family. As a young man he was impressed with the invincible strength of Rome. He believed that God had turned his face away from the Jews and was now blessing the Romans. When Josephus, as military commander of the Jews, surrendered to the Roman general, Vespasian, he claimed that he did so not out of cowardice or lack of devotion to his people, but because of his "divine mission," which was to reveal to Vespasian that he and his son Titus would become emperors of Rome. His veneration for these two Flavian emperors inspired him to romanize his name to Flavius Josephus.

Josephus wrote his account of the Jewish war primarily for Roman readers. Living in Rome under the patronage of the emperors, he wrote a history that would not offend his benefactors. Yet despite his obligations to Rome, Josephus' essential pride in his people and his admiration for their courage and fighting spirit shines through all the pages. No matter how Roman his name, Josephus remained always a Jew.

Shirley Glubok

INTRODUCTION

In the first century A.D., the Empire of Rome, sprawling ponderously across the known world, found itself engaged in a titanic struggle (66–73 A.D.) in Judea, a tiny province along the Mediterranean Sea in the East. After four bloody years, the land lay ravaged. Jerusalem and the Holy Temple smoldered in ruins. It took another three years for events to march the rest of the tragic way to Masada, where the last desperate outposts of resistance were wiped out. Rome, the mightiest military power the world had ever seen, should have been able to put down the first signs of revolt with a local garrison. Instead, the Jews routed one Roman legion and held off three additional legions for three bitter years. According to one count, eighty thousand Roman troops were needed to put down thirty thousand defenders.

  Inevitably, Roman military power, its colossal might pitted against a relatively unarmed people, was victorious. The unequal

Augustus, founder of the Julio-Claudian line of Emperors.
BRITISH MUSEUM

struggle mystified most Roman historians, who subsequently glossed over it in passing, probably because Roman prowess had not been shown in its best light. But the Jewish war changed the course of history for Rome. The line of emperors descending from Julius and Augustus Caesar was displaced, and soon after, Vespasian, the Roman commander in Judea, ascended the throne. Most significantly, the spirit of revolt against Rome was never again completely extinguished.

The story of this Roman-Jewish war was told by the Roman-Jewish historian, Flavius Josephus, whose works are the most comprehensive studies extant of Roman and Jewish life in the century before and the century after the dawn of the Christian era. Josephus wrote his chronicle, entitled *The Jewish War,* around the year 75 A.D., soon after the battles were over. During the nineteen hundred years since, he has been a subject of interest and controversy. In the Middle Ages, Crusaders used a Latin version of Josephus as a guide book to the Holy Land. As recently as a century ago, according to one writer, most households in England could be expected to have a translation of Josephus alongside the family Bible. To his Jewish compatriots Josephus was considerably less than a hero. Turncoat, traitor, opportunist, and braggart are a few of the epithets which have been applied to him through the years. Scholars praise his style and admire his storytelling power, but they cautiously withhold judgment on the authenticity of his historical findings.

The fanatic intensity of the Jewish war was not easy for the Romans to understand. Throughout their entire history, the Jews had shown a determination to worship their one God in

DETAIL FROM A MOSAIC FOUND AT POMPEII.

Alexander the Great defeating the Persians in 333 B.C.
NATIONAL MUSEUM, NAPLES.
ALINARI ART REFERENCE BUREAU

their own way, without idols and forbidden graven images. Frequently during that history, foreign rulers had unsuccessfully attempted to impose different ways upon them. It is probable, however, that the Roman governors, sent to rule this minor province, knew nothing of the historic background of the Jews. One can only imagine their utter bewilderment when confronted with a people who preferred to fight and die rather than allow in their midst the grand marble statuary of which Rome was so proud.

By the time Rome had become the dominant power in the East, the Jews of Judea had survived the rule of the Babylonians, the Persians, the Macedonians, the Egyptians, and the Syrians: Nebuchadnezzar of Babylon had destroyed the Temple of Solomon and taken the Jews into exile; Cyrus of Persia had permitted them to return to Jerusalem because there was little tribute to be had from an empty land; Alexander the Great of Macedon had swept through the country, and many Jews had rallied to him in order to help him conquer Egypt. After Alexander's death, his followers carved up his empire. The Ptolemies took Egypt, and the Seleucids became the rulers of Syria, with their capital at Antioch.

For the next hundred years and more these two powers fought over the trade routes and the tribute of the lands between them. Here were Idumaea, Judea, Samaria, Galilee, and Phoenicia, which were sometimes lumped together and called Palestine. For most of that period the Ptolemies of Egypt controlled Judea.

In the wake of Alexander's conquests, all the wonder of

Alexander introduced an international currency in his Asian conquests, which helped spread the influence of Hellenism.
BRITISH MUSEUM

Greek thought and culture flowed into Asia. The Greek language became widespread as the voice of commerce and government. Greek culture surrounded the Jews on all sides and its philosophical and artistic attractions tempted many hearts. Young Jews were drawn to Hellenism's stress on physical perfection, and older men pondered its rationalities and its world outlook. Although the wealthier, more powerful classes were openly tolerant of the new Hellenistic ways, every effort to impose these customs and beliefs by force produced the same result: a fierce resistance against all odds, no matter how overpowering.

The area that was known then as Judea cannot be described geographically with exactitude. Its boundaries kept changing. A thousand years before the time of Josephus, when David and Solomon ruled over the united Jewish kingdoms of Judah and Israel, the territory was at its greatest. After Solomon, the kingdoms broke apart in bickering rivalry and the boundaries shrank.

After the exile in Babylon, the Jews returned to Jerusalem and continued following their ancestral customs and laws, ruled by their own High Priests. Foreign overlords were content to exact their tribute and leave well enough alone. Early in the second century B.C., the main struggle in the East was between Syria and Egypt, with Rome just beginning to make its presence felt. The Seleucids of Syria had wrested the rule of Judea from Egypt; and the Jews, undisturbed at first in their traditional way of life, accepted their new conquerors quietly. Syrian rule, however, proved feeble; the rivalries with Egypt continued unabated; and the Jews, as a consequence, found a new national spirit awakening in their hearts. It did not take long before there were direct, open conflicts with their Hellenized masters.

Josephus' chronicle of the Jewish war begins at this point in the history of his people—about two hundred years before the actual outbreak of hostilities with Rome—when the Seleucid monarch, Antiochus IV Epiphanes, found himself balked by Rome, by a dwindling treasury, and by his Jewish subjects, who refused to accept a uniform Hellenistic code in common with all other peoples under Syrian sway. Antiochus savagely put down revolt in Jerusalem, selling thousands of its people into slavery and massacring many of the rest. He occupied the Holy Temple and set up idols of a Greek god, whose features curiously resembled his own. The Syrian tyrant put a stop to all Jewish religious observances and ordered instead profane sacrifices on the altars. Jewish traditions were outlawed throughout the land: the observance of the Sabbath and the circumcision of male children were forbidden. Rites and sacrifices, which outraged Jewish religious sensibilities, were made mandatory for everyone. The Jews resisted Antiochus, who made the mistake of resorting to force to impose his will. The result was that even his followers were pushed into armed rebellion. Three years after Antiochus profaned the Holy Temple, he was driven out by Judas Maccabaeus, who cleansed and reconsecrated the sacred building, an event memorialized ever since in the Festival of Hanukkah. The holy war against Antiochus was first led by Judas' father, whose family, the Hasmoneans, became the ruling and later the royal family of the Jews. Judas' brother, Simon, finally expelled the last invader from Judea and the land was free from foreign dominations for the first time in almost two hundred years.

For much of this time, Rome, still occupied in the West, remained a shadowy but threatening presence in the East. But Rome was concerned with the ambitions of the Syrian Empire and interested in any possibility of keeping it weak and in turmoil. Roman threats had checked Seleucid hopes of conquest on several occasions, and Judas Maccabaeus had turned to Rome for an alliance against Antiochus IV Epiphanes. Judas' successors renewed the treaty with Rome, but the alliance remained generally inoperative. In 139 B.C., during the rule of Simon, the Roman Senate recognized the independence of Judea.

Simon's son, John Hyrcanus (134–104 B.C.), launched a new era of conquest and expansion. With Simon's grandsons, Jewish kings were again installed on Jewish thrones. Alexander Jannaeus (103–76 B.C.) surrounded himself with an opulent court, dazzling with pomp and luxury. In many ways, the new Jewish sovereigns adopted the trappings of the Hellenistic monarchies. With hired mercenaries they conquered and annexed territories such as Idumaea (Biblical Edom) and Galilee, whose inhabitants were converted to Judaism. But even though there was often open bitterness between the crown and the people, the basic beliefs and traditions of the Jews remained inviolate. The kings built great palaces and fortresses in Judea, but they never decorated them with forbidden images. No coinage circulating in Judea bore the likenesses of the Jewish rulers.

The rule of the Hasmoneans over Judea reached what is called its golden era during the reign of Queen Alexandra (78–69

B.C.). For a few years the land was prosperous and comparatively at peace. The popular sect of the Pharisees became the dominating influence on the Queen, instead of the aristocratic, priestly Sadducees, who had held power with previous Jewish rulers. The Sadducees comprised the wealthier, worldly landowning class, too often interested only in maintaining its own privileges. The Sadducees represented the conservative tendency in Jewish religious thought, holding the written Scripture as the sole basis for Jewish law. The Pharisees, who represented the overwhelming majority of the people, believed that oral tradition also provided binding authority to change laws and customs. There was a third sect among the Jews, the Essenes, who preferred to withdraw into a monastic life, where they devoted themselves to manual labor, study, prayer, and acts of benevolence.

Queen Alexandra's sons were at each other's throats, even before she died. The dispossessed Sadducees rallied around Alexandra's younger son, Aristobulus. Alexandra's elder son, Hyrcanus, was named by his mother to be High Priest of the Jews, an office no woman could hold. He accepted foreign support, supplied by the intrigues of a noble Idumaean, named Antipater, founder of the power-hungry family which came to be known as the Herodians, after Antipater's son King Herod the Great.

While Alexandra's sons were fighting over the throne in Jerusalem, Rome was finally on the march in Asia. Under the command of Pompey the Great, Roman arms swept from one conquest to another. Pompey intervened in Judea, taking ad-

Pompey the Great

Julius Caesar

vantage of the bloody rivalry of the Jewish princes. Supporting the claims of Hyrcanus against Aristobulus' partisans, Pompey assaulted and captured the Holy Temple in Jerusalem, although he wisely left it unmolested. But he did take away Hyrcanus' crown, leaving him only with the hereditary title of High Priest. The territories conquered by the early Hasmonean kings were detached and most of Judea was merged into the newly established Roman province of Syria. The brief independence of the Jews was over.

But Rome was also at war with itself. The opposing rivals for supreme power bled the provinces for tribute to support the expensive conflict. The contenders for the Jewish throne took advantage of the confusion and sought allies now in this camp, now in that. All the great names of Roman history appear on the scene in the battles around Judea. Hyrcanus, at first aligned

Silver cup, with head representing Cleopatra.
TREASURE OF BOSCOREALE. LOUVRE
ALINARI ART REFERENCE BUREAU

with Pompey, swung over to Julius Caesar, when Pompey was defeated in 48 B.C. Julius Caesar confirmed Hyrcanus in his religious role, but he gave the crafty Antipater a clear field to take over the actual rule of Judea. Antipater immediately named his sons to the highest posts in the land. Herod became governor of Galilee, where he came to the attention of the Roman leaders, particularly Mark Antony. Antony sponsored Herod as King of Judea in 40 B.C., with the support of Augustus Caesar. Three years later, with the help of a Roman legion, Herod stormed Jerusalem, captured the Temple, and established his claim to the throne. When the war between Antony and Augustus was decided in favor of the latter in 31 B.C., Herod tendered his loyalty to the winner. Augustus accepted his services as a client king and even enlarged the territory over which Herod was given the rule.

Herod was dynamic and forceful. He was also jealous, suspicious, and cruel. He was king of Judea for thirty-four years and glorified his reign with public works which were the wonders of the world. Josephus describes many of them, listing the cities and palaces which Herod built as memorials to himself, his family and friends. Herod created a seaport on the Mediterranean, building it out of gleaming white limestone and filling it with palaces, temples, gymnasia, fountains, theatres, amphitheatres, and hippodromes. He called it Caesarea in honor of the Emperor in Rome. He turned rock mountains in the desert into royal hideaways and fortresses, which were designed to give him shelter both from his Jewish subjects and from Cleopatra, Queen of Egypt, who made no pretense of concealing her desire to

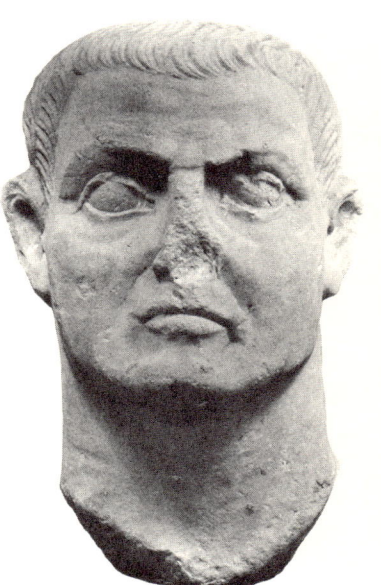

Mark Antony

Tiberius

repossess the land her ancestors had ruled. Chief of these desert fortresses was Masada, a bleak rock plateau overlooking the Dead Sea, where Herod built the three-tiered palace and the huge armories and storehouses which were recently excavated by archaeologists.

Herod spent many years restoring the Holy Temple in Jerusalem. He erected new foundation walls, doubled the area the Temple occupied, and set around it wondrous columns and courtyards. Thousands of men were put to work building the magnificent structure. Herod also rebuilt the fortress north of the Temple, outfitted it luxuriously, and named it Antonia in honor of his friend, Mark Antony.

King Herod tried to strengthen his own ties with the Jewish royal family of the Hasmoneans by marrying Mariamme, a granddaughter of the High Priest Hyrcanus. But Herod's suspicious nature was reflected in his court, which was racked with conspiracy and intrigue, inspired by his eldest son, Antipater. Herod could not rest easy as long as a single member of the Hasmonean family lived to threaten his right to the throne. He ordered the execution of his royal wife, Mariamme, in 29 B.C. His two sons by Mariamme were condemned for plotting against their father's life and were strangled. Herod himself died in 4 B.C., having had ten wives and fifteen children. At his death, his kingdom was divided among three of his sons, Archelaus, Herod Antipas, and Philip. Archelaus was given sway over Judea, but he proved a brutal ruler and was deposed after ten years. Herod Antipas, whose name appears in the early chronicles of Christianity, founded a city on the shores of the Sea of Galilee,

which he named Tiberias in honor of the new emperor of Rome. Philip founded a city which he named Caesarea. It became known also as Caesarea-Philippi to distinguish it from the Caesarea built by his father on the Mediterranean.

Judea became an imperial province after Archelaus was deposed. Roman governors, called procurators, were sent by the emperors to rule the province, collect the tribute, and oversee the affairs of the Empire. Some of the procurators looked even more diligently after their own affairs and fortunes.

About this time, a man named Judah appeared in Galilee, loudly berating his countrymen for accepting the yoke of Rome when they already had as their master the God of the Jews. Many

The "Gemma Augustus," an onyx cameo, shows Augustus Caesar being crowned with laurel.
KUNSTHISTORISCHES MUSEUM, VIENNA

Caligula

people flocked to him and formed a new Jewish sect called the Zealots. They were fierce partisans of Jewish independence. As war with Rome grew inevitable, the ranks of the Zealots swelled with recruits from all other segments of Jewish life. Josephus could never bring himself to acknowledge these passionate defenders of Jewish liberty, whom he labeled brigands, outlaws, bandits, and robbers. It was these Zealots who bore the brunt of the war, which they almost won. It was the Zealots, too, who brought the final curtain down during the tragic night on Masada.

One of the earliest of the Roman procurators was the unpopular Pontius Pilate, who tried to force the people of Jerusalem to accept the presence of Roman battle standards within the city walls. These devices, which were carried into battle by every Roman legion, were carved with graven images, including elaborate portraits of the emperor. Pilate withdrew these standards when the people calmly offered to die rather than permit such a violation of their oldest traditions. Other procurators were prudent enough not to antagonize the sensibilities of the proud and stubborn people, and they enjoyed comparative peace. Roman procurators were ruling in Judea in 37 A.D., when Joseph ben Matthias was born in Jerusalem. He was to become the historian of his times, Flavius Josephus.

That same year a new emperor ascended the throne in Rome. His name was Gaius, generally known as Caligula. Also that year a child was born into the imperial family in Rome and named Nero.

Caligula managed in a few short years to stir up enough

OPPOSITE:
The Roman army's Praetorian Guard forced the Senate to accept Claudius as Emperor.
LOUVRE. ALINARI

Agrippa I

animosity to insure his assassination. One of his more maniacal impulses was to proclaim his own divinity and to order public worship of his portraits throughout the Empire. In Judea there was consternation and fury. Caligula's orders were backed by all the armed might of Rome, and the war might have started then but for the death of Caligula.

Herod's grandson, Agrippa, was in Rome seeking to win back his family's position and fortune in Judea. The young prince was a frequent visitor at the court of the elderly emperor, Tiberius. He was an intimate companion of Caligula. He helped swing the transfer of imperial power to Claudius in 41 A.D. His reward came in his restoration to the throne of his grandfather as Agrippa I. For four years (41–44 A.D.), a king of Jewish stock ruled again in Jerusalem. These events must have made strong impressions on the mind of young Josephus, growing up in that city. There was much building activity as Agrippa sought to reinforce the city walls. The building of the Holy Temple continued until 64 A.D., just six short years before its destruction.

When Agrippa I died, his young son, Marcus Julius Agrippa, was not named to the throne in Jerusalem. Later, when the young prince came of age, he was installed by Emperor Claudius on the throne of several small provinces around the Sea of Galilee as Agrippa II. He was also given the right to oversee the affairs of the Temple in Jerusalem and to appoint the High Priest. He was, therefore, a frequent visitor to Jerusalem, where he was often accompanied by his sister, Berenice.

After Agrippa I died, rule by procurator was re-established in Judea, and the antagonisms between Roman and Jew began slowly to mount. During the rule of the procurator, Cumanus, 48–52 A.D., bitterness between the Jews and Romans grew in intensity. Josephus describes the insolence of one Roman soldier, which drove Jerusalem into a frenzy and led to bloodshed. During the Feast of Passover, when the city overflowed with pilgrims, the Romans, as was their practice, stationed a detachment of soldiers in the courtyard of the Temple, supposedly to keep the peace. One soldier, on an overhanging roof, turned his backside to the crowd, lifted up his robes and outraged the people by making a noise as insulting as his posture. Cumanus, the procurator, tried to smooth over the situation but the crowd would not be calmed. The procurator called for reinforcements, and a crushing panic ensued in the jammed streets and courtyards. Josephus estimated the bloody toll that day at twenty thousand lives.

But it was just the beginning. A Roman slave was robbed on the highway outside of Jerusalem, and the procurator ordered all nearby towns punished for failing to capture the thieves. In one retaliatory raid, a Roman soldier found a scroll of sacred Jewish scripture, tore it in half, and tossed it contemptuously into a fire. Almost as one man, the Jews of city and country rose up and demanded that the offending soldier be punished. There was no way to quiet this fury, and the Roman was surrendered to the populace for punishment. The young Josephus might very well have been aware of the bloody revenge taken by the people on the unfortunate Roman. Cumanus was finally recalled by the Emperor Claudius and banished.

Claudius' next appointment as procurator of Judea was a

Claudius portrayed as Jupiter. The realistic treatment of the head contrasts with the idealized body.
VATICAN MUSEUM. ANDERSON

man of low station, brother of a freed slave who had become one of the Emperor's most trusted advisors. The new procurator, Marcus Antonius Felix, ruled for eight years (52–60 A.D.), a period which saw an ominous hardening in the rebellious spirit of the Jews. Previously, Jewish revolts had flared from time to time but had subsided. Under Felix, rebellion became the overriding mood of the country. Very soon it exploded into the open hostilities of the Jewish war.

Josephus' historical prelude to the outbreak of the Jewish war in 66 A.D. occupies one and a half books of the original work's total of seven. The condensed and rewritten version in the preceding pages has the same purpose: to fill in the background of the war, with its panorama of events and people, many of whom are already familiar to modern readers.

Abridging and adapting the Josephus work for twentieth century reading poses several dilemmas. Josephus wrote his history in the first century of our era, when historians employed highly stylized conventions. One of these is the attribution of oratorical statements to principals in the history, under conditions which would have made verbatim transcriptions difficult if not impossible. But this device, which rings so strangely in modern ears, could not have been eliminated entirely without weakening the noble poetry of the final hours of the war—the heroic martyrdom of the last defenders of Masada.

In modernizing Josephus' story, however, some of his discursiveness had to be trimmed away in favor of the more direct story of the war. The power of the historical drama thus stands out more clearly. The formal language has been modified and the narrative personalized by letting Josephus refer to himself consistently in the first person. (In the original he alternated between a first and a third person usage.) Modern dating has been inserted, though Josephus' calendar is referred to from time to time to retain the flavor of his text.

This version of *The Jewish War* is intended to make more accessible to readers of all ages one of the great historical sources of both Jewish and Roman life in the early days of our era.

The Roman Empire: First Century A.D.

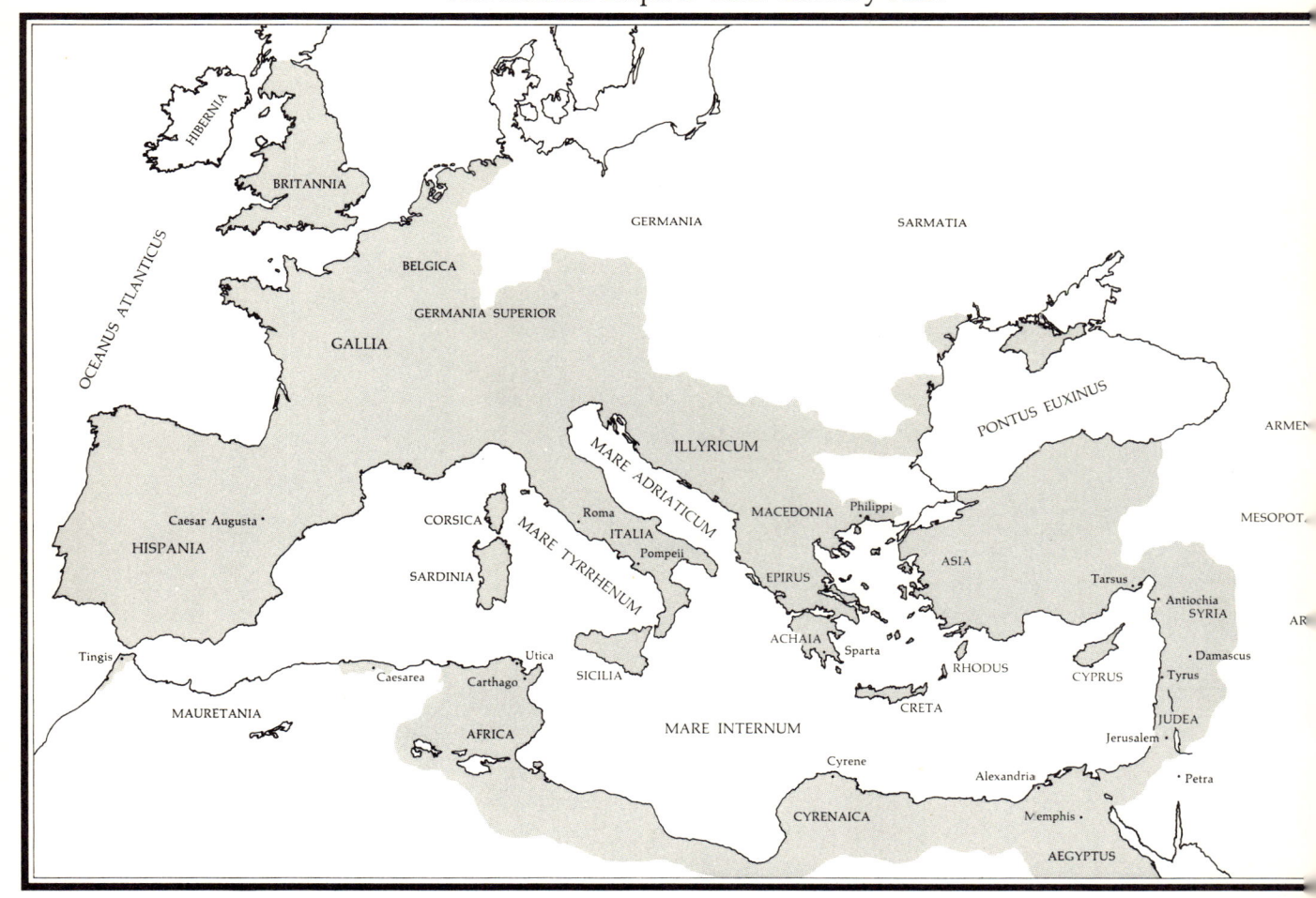

It can renew acquaintance with one of the great military conflicts of history and it can provide greater depth to the understanding of the period through the use of illustrative material, both ancient and modern—the assembling of which also posed a dilemma. As has been pointed out, the Jewish war was fought at least in part over the issue of the forbidden graven images. How then to depict the Jewish side of the war, when faced with a total absence of graphic representations of kings, generals, armies, weapons, cities, peoples, and the like? On the Roman side, of course, the situation is reversed. There is an abundance of statues and coins portraying the Caesars. The Arch of Titus in Rome, celebrating a somewhat dubious triumph, is still standing, with its relief panels showing Jewish prisoners and the spoils from the Temple. Therefore, illustrations from many Roman sources have been used to dramatize the events of Josephus' history.

Interest in Josephus and his writings has increased recently, not only because of his story of the war and of the Masada epic, but because he provided descriptions in great detail of the Judea and Jerusalem of his day. These descriptions have become an important source for a model-sized reconstruction of the city of Jerusalem at the time of the Second Temple. Built by a team of archaeologists, artists, sculptors, and model-makers, the scale city is now almost completed on the grounds of the Holyland Hotel near Jerusalem. Photographs of the walls, towers, palaces, even of the Holy Sanctuary itself, reconstructed to scale, as they probably existed nineteen hundred years ago, make a vivid accompaniment to Josephus' text. Where appropriate, archaeological views of the fortress at Masada, the relics of the Zealots which were found, and the remains of the Roman encampment which can still be seen have been included.

There is a vast library of scholarship about Josephus, much of it controversial. In view of the resurgent interest in his work, there will probably be much more said on every side of the questions which surround his name. No attempt has been made here to summarize any of this scholarly literature or to deal with the many problems of inconsistency in Josephus' reporting. Many of Josephus' statistics are, to say the least, open to question. For the full, formal text, completely annotated, the reader is referred to the translation by H. St. J. Thackeray in the Loeb Classical Library edition. Like the Greek text, on which the translation was based, this abridgment contains none of the controversial Christian references which are attributed to Josephus in *Antiquities*—a later work—and in the Old Slavonic versions of the *War*. Grateful appreciation is given to the Harvard University Press for making the H. St. J. Thackeray translation available for this version. Thanks are due also to John A. Pope, Jr., who encouraged the development of this book and helped see it through all stages of preparation; to Miss Margaret R. Scherer, Research Fellow at the Metropolitan Museum of Art, for valuable suggestions from her vast knowledge of Roman art; and to Ernest Nash, for his advice and guidance.

CHRONOLOGY

B.C.

c. 1010–973	Reign of King David. Jerusalem conquered and made the capital of the kingdoms of Judah and Israel
c. 974–937	Reign of King Solomon. The First Temple is built
586	Nebuchadnezzar of Babylon conquers Judea and destroys the Temple
538	Cyrus of Persia conquers Babylon and grants return of Jews to Jerusalem
515	Second Temple finished in Jerusalem
333–323	Alexander the Great conquers Persia and rules Judea
323–198	Ptolemies of Egypt rule in Judea
198	Seleucids of Syria win rule over Judea
166–165	Judas Maccabaeus defeats Seleucids, cleanses and reconsecrates the Temple (Hannukah)
142	Judea, freed of invaders, is independent
141	Hasmonean High Priesthood established
105–63	Hasmonean kings rule Judea
63	Pompey captures Jerusalem. Judea under Roman rule
48–44	Julius Caesar, ruler of Rome
37–4	Rule of Herod the Great in Judea
30	Augustus Caesar. Establishment of Roman Empire

B.C.

4	Herod's sons, Archelaus, Herod Antipas, and Philip, divide his kingdom

A.D.

6	Judea becomes a Roman province Resistance begins with formation of Zealot sect
14–37	Tiberius, Emperor of Rome
c. 26–36	Pontius Pilate named procurator of Judea
c. 30	Crucifixion of Jesus
37	Birth of Josephus
37–41	Gaius Caligula, Emperor of Rome
41–54	Claudius, Emperor of Rome
41–44	Agrippa I, grandson of Herod the Great, King of Judea
44	Rule of Roman procurators resumes
54–68	Nero, Emperor of Rome
66	Roman-Jewish War begins
67	Vespasian takes command of the Roman forces
68–69	The Year of the Four Emperors—Galba, Otho, Vitellius, Vespasian
69–79	Vespasian, Emperor of Rome
70	Titus destroys the Second Temple and captures Jerusalem
73	Fall of Masada
79	Pompeii buried by Mt. Vesuvius
79–81	Titus, Emperor of Rome
81–96	Domitian, Emperor of Rome
c. 100	Death of Josephus
116–117	Jewish rebellions put down by Emperor Trajan
132–135	Revolt in Judea against Rome under Simon bar-Kochba
476	Fall of the Roman Empire

I

The war of the Jews against the Romans—the greatest war of our times and, according to some accounts, the fiercest ever fought between cities or nations—has not lacked historians. But too much of what has been written is secondhand; too much contradictory, written as flattery for the Romans or out of spite for the Jews. I, Josephus, son of Matthias, a Jew born in Jerusalem, a member of a priestly family, fought the Romans at the beginning of the war and later observed the war as a prisoner of the Romans. Therefore, I can provide the people of the Roman world with the true facts. I have no intention of making the Roman victory seem greater by exaggerating the heroism of my compatriots. I shall faithfully recount the actions of both sides, but I will not try to hide my personal feelings, nor hold back my sympathy for the misfortune that befell my country.

However, if there is anyone who must find fault with me for my harsh words about the leaders of my people, or for my grief over my country's tragic fate, I beg forgiveness for these emotions, which really are outside the province of the historian. If there be any critic who will not permit such emotions, let him give history the credit for the facts, and the historian the blame for the grief.

October, 54 A.D. When Nero ascended the throne, he confirmed the appointment of Felix, whom his stepfather had named procurator of Judea. Felix was then engaged on a campaign of clearing the countryside of roving bands of brigands, who were ravaging the land. He succeeded in capturing one important rebel chief, named Eleazar, who for twenty years had pillaged the country. Felix sent him, with many of his men, as prisoners to Rome. He crucified many other insurgents who fell into his hands and punished countless numbers of common people who were charged with being in league with the marauders.

But while he was successfully clearing the country, a new kind of resistance was springing up in the city of Jerusalem: the *sicarii*, or "curved daggers," so named after the deadly weapons which they carried hidden under their clothing. These outlaws committed murders in broad daylight in the very heart of the city, particularly during the Festivals. They escaped detection by mingling swiftly with the crowds and joining in with loud cries of outrage and indignation at the daring assassinations. In addition, other disturbances arose among the people. False prophets appeared and led the people astray with promises of deliverance from Rome. Felix mercilessly set his soldiers upon them and put many of them and their followers to the sword.

59–60 A.D. At this time, too, the tension between the Jewish inhabitants of Caesarea and the Syrian portion of the population reached a breaking point. The Jews claimed the right to rule the city on the ground that it had been founded by a Jew, King Herod. The Syrians admitted the Jewish origin of Herod, but maintained that he had built it for the Syrian Greeks since he had filled it with temples and statues which were forbidden to the Jews. Feelings between the two peoples ran higher and higher, and blood often flowed. Felix tried to stop the bloody struggle, but he really was prejudiced in favor of the Syrians. Since he could find no way to settle the quarrel, Felix decided to send the leading men of both communities to Rome to plead their causes before Nero.

Soon thereafter Felix was succeeded as procurator of Judea by Festus, who continued to pursue the brigands, the chief curse of the country. Festus, in turn, was succeeded by Albinus, whose administration was of quite another order. Albinus was greedy and rapacious. He plundered and stole, accepted secret bribes and ransoms, but even his excesses were nothing compared to the actions of Gessius Florus, who followed him as procurator. Florus boasted openly of his own outrages against the nation. He was unbelievably cruel, with utter contempt for truth. He did not bother to cheat single individuals. He stripped whole cities, ruined whole populations, virtually granting a free hand to any villainy just as long as he was cut in for a share of the plunder. On one occasion, during the Feast of Unleavened Bread, when Cestius Gallus, governor of Syria, was visiting Jerusalem, the Jews crowded around him and denounced Florus and his crimes. But Florus scoffed at the accusations. He was

Nero, portrayed as Apollo.
VATICAN MUSEUM. ANDERSON

60–62 A.D.
62–64 A.D.

64 A.D.

65 A.D.

already toying with the idea of starting open warfare upon the whole nation—his only hope of diverting attention from his own wrongdoings. Florus reasoned that, if peace continued, the Jews sooner or later would accuse him before Caesar. But if he could incite a revolt, the larger catastrophe would forestall any inquiry into his lesser offenses. Florus, intent on provoking this revolt, doubled the sufferings of the people every day.

Meanwhile the Syrians of Caesarea had won their case at Nero's court and received from him the rule of the city. It was *c. May, 66 A.D.* here in fact that the war broke out, in the twelfth year of Nero's reign and the seventeenth year of Agrippa's.

Florus took every opportunity to fan the flames of war. He scorned any appeals for help or justice and often threw the supplicants into prison. He looted the sacred treasury of the Temple, pretending it was required by the Emperor, which provoked the people into passionate outcries for liberation from his misrule. Some malcontents ridiculed Florus' avarice by passing a hat around, begging coppers for him as though he were destitute. Florus, instead of going to Caesarea to extinguish the conflagration that was breaking out there—as he was being paid to do—marched on Jerusalem with an army of cavalry and infantry. The people tried to shame Florus with signs of friendliness, but the procurator responded with a furious order to his soldiers to sack the Upper Market in Jerusalem and to kill everyone in sight. The ensuing massacre was appalling, totalling 3,600, including women and children, for even babes in arms received no mercy. Florus went so far that day as to scourge and crucify men, who, though Jews by birth, had been honored by the Romans with the rank of knight. Even the personal appeal of Queen Berenice, Agrippa's sister, who was in Jerusalem on a religious pilgrimage, had no effect on Florus. The mad fury of the soldiers almost overwhelmed the queen, endangering her life. She managed to escape by slipping into the Royal Palace just in time.

Feeling in Jerusalem against Florus kept mounting and mounting, despite the efforts of the influential citizens and the chief priests to keep the people calm. But Florus did not want peace. He poured fresh fuel on the flames by calling for more troops from Caesarea and by provoking a pitched battle on the outskirts of Jerusalem, in which many fell under the blows of the Romans. Inside the city Florus led his soldiers in another attack, but he was beaten back to the palace before he could reach the fortress of Antonia, which was connected to the Temple. To prevent his reaching the Temple through the fortress, the Jewish revolutionaries cut a gap in the connecting passage. This action made Florus pause. He decided to quit Jerusalem, but to keep the war fever high he sent false reports to the Roman governor in Syria, accusing the Jews of starting the fighting and charging them with violence of which they were really the victims. But the Jewish leaders in Jerusalem and Queen Berenice, too, sent many dispatches to Syria, reporting the outrageous conduct of Florus. Cestius, the governor, decided to send an officer, a tribune named Neapolitanus, to learn the truth about the state of affairs in Judea. King Agrippa, who was on his way home from Alexandria, met Neapolitanus on the outskirts of Jerusalem. Together they listened to the accounts

June 3, 66 A.D.

Poppea, wife of Nero
CAPITOLINE MUSEUM, ROME. ANDERSON

of Florus' brutalities. Neapolitanus was persuaded to make a tour of the city without any bodyguards, just to test the loyalty of the population. He observed the burnt and plundered houses and the wrecked market place. He moved about with only a single attendant and saw that the Jews were loyal to all Roman officials, with the sole exception of Florus, the procurator. Neapolitanus then called all the people together, commended them highly on their loyalty to Rome, and urged them strongly to keep the peace. Whereupon he returned to report to Cestius in Syria.

Now the people begged Agrippa and the chief priests to send an embassy to Nero to denounce Florus as the real aggressor. King Agrippa, realizing how dangerous the mood of the people was, called them together and addressed them, while his sister, Berenice, looked on from the roof of the royal palace of the Hasmoneans. Agrippa pointed out the terrible horrors that war entailed and urged the Jews to realize that all their fury against one Roman did not justify a war against Rome. He counseled submission and patience, and went on to say that all calls for independence and liberty were too late. He pointed to all the world, from Athens, Sparta, Macedon, to Asia, Thrace, Illyria, Dalmatia, Gaul, Spain, Germany, and even Britain, all under the sway of Rome. Agrippa warned that a war with Rome would bring fearful destruction on the people and the land. The Holy Places would be destroyed. Finally he begged the people to cherish all the blessings of peace, which he would gladly share with them. But he solemnly warned them that they would not have his support if they kept on calling for war.

The Romans collect tribute.
TRIER MUSEUM FOTOTECA UNIONE

King Agrippa went even further and pointed out that the Jews were already in a state of revolt because they had stopped paying tribute to Rome and had cut down the passage connecting the Temple and the lower fortress of Antonia—an act of war. The people quickly accepted Agrippa's advice and began to rebuild the passage. They also rushed men to the neighboring villages to collect tribute. But when Agrippa tried to persuade the people to keep submitting to Florus until he was replaced by Nero, the Jews lost their tempers, abused the king, and proclaimed his banishment from Jerusalem. Some hotheads even had the audacity to throw stones at him. Agrippa, convinced now that passions were out of control, withdrew to his own kingdom.

Now some of the fiercest firebrands for war banded together and assaulted the fortress of Masada, captured the stronghold, and slew the Roman guards, replacing them with a garrison of their own. At the same time, certain officials of the Holy Temple in Jerusalem took it upon themselves to stop accepting gifts and offerings from foreigners, with the result that no sacrifices continued for Rome or for Caesar. War with Rome was getting closer and closer, but even so the Jews were not all in agreement. The chief priests begged the Temple priests to restore the ceremonies of sacrifice for the Romans, but their pleas fell on deaf ears. Some of the leading citizens, fearful of the wrath of Rome, sent deputations to Florus and to Agrippa, beseeching them to move on Jerusalem in force before the revolt grew completely out of control. This news delighted Florus, who regarded it as heaven-sent and did not even bother to reply.

Agrippa, concerned for his compatriots, eager to keep Rome from losing Judea and the Jews from losing Jerusalem and the Temple, sent two thousand horsemen to the city.

c. August, 66 A.D.

Inside Jerusalem the struggle between the elements who favored peace with Rome and the parties who clamored for rebellion went on for seven days. On the eighth, a feast day devoted to bringing up wood to the Temple for the Holy Altar, the rebels, joined by the insurgents, dislodged the troops of Agrippa from the Upper City. They put the king's palace to the torch and burned down the public archives, thus winning over the poor and impoverished, whose records of debts had gone up in flames. The following day, the rebels attacked the fortress of Antonia, and after a two-day siege, captured the garrison, massacred it, and set fire to the fortress. Then they laid siege to the palace, where Agrippa's men and the pro-Roman citizens had fled for refuge. The battle continued without letup, day and night.

At this moment, one Menahem, a descendant of the founder of the sect of the Zealots, rushed to Masada with a group of friends and broke open the armory which Herod had established there years before, and acquired thus a supply of weapons for his fellows and for the other insurgents. He rushed back to Jerusalem and was joyfully received, like a king, and given command of the forces besieging the palace. With new spirit, the attackers undermined the walls of the palace, which collapsed. The beleaguered garrison sought a truce to quit the building. This was granted, but only to Agrippa's troops and to Jewish nationals, who came out accordingly. The Romans, left without allies, were ashamed to sue for terms. They retired to more strongly fortified towers and strongholds, but not until after Menahem and his men had cut down any stragglers who did not make their escape quickly enough.

The next day, however, Menahem decked himself out in kingly robes, revealing his insufferable ambition to rule the Jews. When his rivals saw this, they attacked him and pelted him with stones, till he was driven to flee. One of his closest kin, Eleazar, son of Yair, decided to leave Jerusalem and return to Masada, where he later became the dominating figure. Menahem, too, tried to escape but he was caught hiding, dragged into the open and put to death.

The siege of the Roman garrison continued to be pressed with vigor until the Roman commander, unable to prolong his resistance, offered to surrender all arms and supplies in return for their lives. But, in spite of a treaty of safe conduct, as soon as the Roman troops laid down their shields and swords, they were surrounded and massacred without mercy. The Roman commander, by promising to become a Jew and even to be circumcised, managed to save himself alive.

War with Rome now seemed inevitable. All of Jerusalem gave way to a public display of dejection and mourning. For to add to the awfulness of the event, the massacre had taken place on the Sabbath, a day on which Jews, out of deep religious scruples, refrain from even the most righteous acts. On that very day, at that very hour, as though wrought by the hand of Providence, the people of Caesarea massacred the Jewish population of that city. More than twenty thousand Jews were

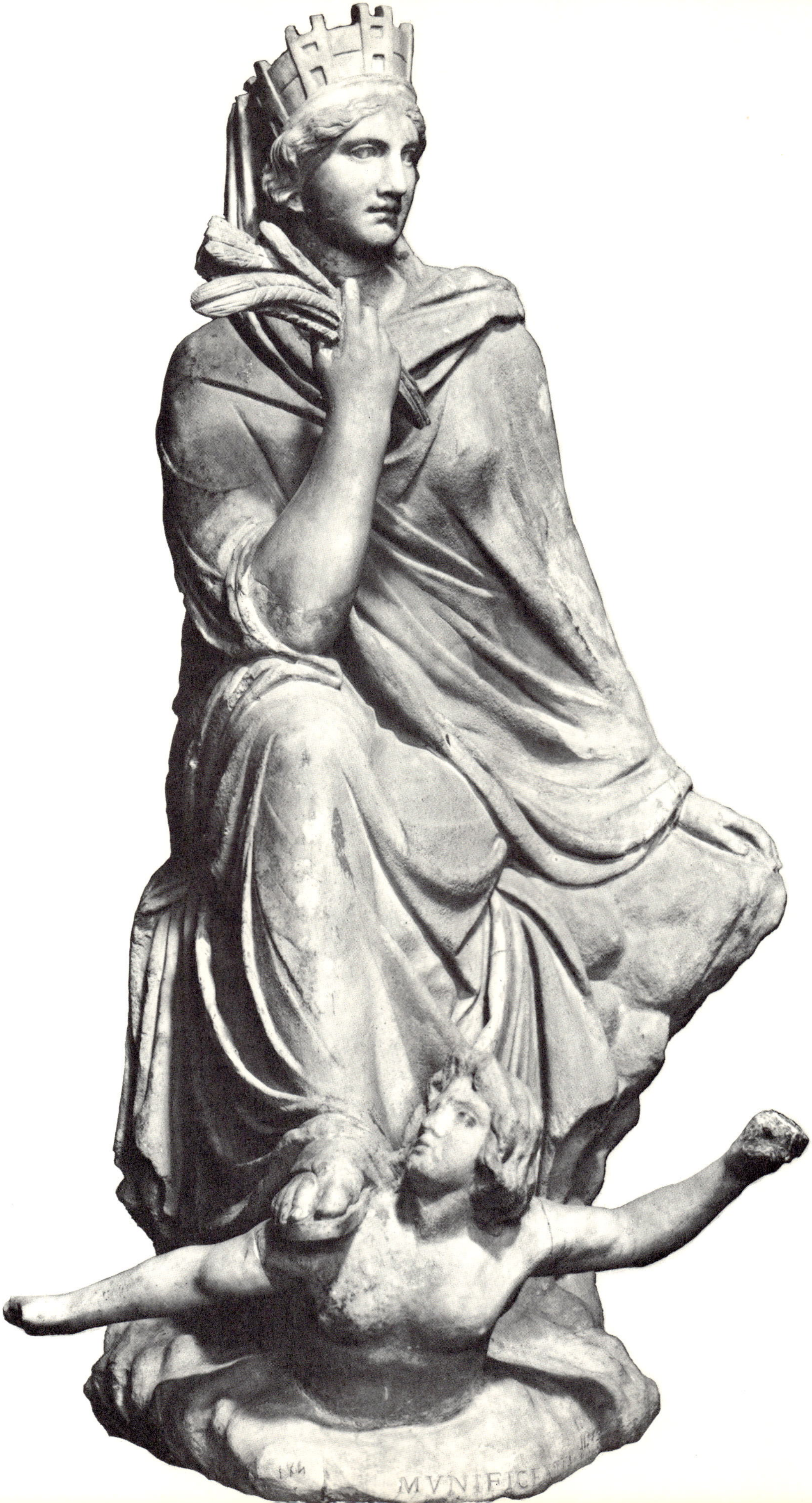
MVNIFICE

slaughtered in less than an hour. The Jews struck back at Syrians throughout the land in reprisal, and the Syrians in turn wreaked vengeance on the Jews in their midst. All through Syria, city after city rose against the Jews and slew them by the thousands. The disturbance reached even to Alexandria in Egypt where an entire quarter of the city called the Delta was occupied by the Jews. Two Roman legions were rushed to the Delta with permission to kill, plunder, and burn, with the result that the district was drowned in the blood of fifty thousand corpses.

With war now being waged on the Jews on all sides, Cestius Gallus, governor of Syria, decided it was time to take some action himself. He marched out of Antioch with the Twelfth Roman Legion in full strength, supported by picked men from other legions and, in addition, six cohorts of infantry and four squadrons of cavalry. Besides these he had auxiliary contingents, consisting of two thousand horsemen and three thousand foot soldiers, all archers, supplied by the north Syrian king Antiochus. He also had an equal number of foot soldiers and rather less than two thousand horsemen, supplied by Agrippa, who came along personally to guide Cestius and to watch out for the interests of his men. The Romans captured several strongholds in Galilee, and the entire province was reduced to submission. Cestius regrouped his armies and moved on Jerusalem, reaching a place called Gibeon, six miles away. Thousands of Jews had assembled in Jersalem for the Feast of Tabernacles, but, seeing the war upon them, they abandoned the Feast and rushed to arms, with so much passion, that they broke through the Romans ranks and put all the invading legion in peril. The Jews occupied the

OPPOSITE:
Antioch, capital of Syria, personified as a crowned woman seated on a mountain. Her foot rests on a figure representing a river god.
VATICAN MUSEUM. ALINARI

high ground surrounding the Romans and were in a position to imperil the entire force. But internal discord broke out amongst the Jews. Cestius seized the favorable moment and attacked. He brought up his whole force, routed the Jews and pursued them to Jerusalem. The Roman governor camped in the region called Scopus, or Lookout Hill, three-quarters of a mile distant from the city.

After waiting in vain for three days for the Jews to capitulate, Cestius deployed his troops and marched into the city. He set up his position in front of the Royal Palace in the Upper City. Had he, at that particular moment, decided to force his way through the walls, he would have captured the city and the war would have been over. But Cestius was diverted by his supply officer and most of his cavalry commanders, who had been bribed by the evil procurator, Florus. For this reason the war went on so long, and the Jews were forced to drink so deeply of the cup of disaster. Cestius could have undermined the walls. After five days of indecisive fighting, the Roman troops reached the north side of the Temple and the first row planted their shields against the wall, the rank behind placed their shields upon the first row, the rows behind doing likewise, so that an armed roof, called "a tortoise," was formed, from which missiles and weapons glanced off harmlessly. The city was in panic. The insurgents began running away in consternation. The moderates tried to open the gates and receive Cestius as their deliverer. Once again, if Cestius had persisted he could have taken the city and ended the war, but God, I suppose, had already turned his back even on His own Sanctuary.

A tablet from the Second Temple in Jerusalem warning foreigners to keep away from the sacred enclosures around the Sanctuary on pain of death.
LOUVRE. GIRAUDON

At any rate, Cestius suddenly called off his troops and, having not really suffered any reverse, pulled back from Jerusalem. The insurgents immediately plucked up courage and sallied forth to the attack, killing off the rear guard, surrounding the moving column on either side, and taking a heavy toll. The Romans kept tight ranks, while the Jews, lightly armed, dashed in and out among them. The Roman legion staggered back to its camp at Gibeon, having lost many men and officers, and most of its supplies and equipment. Cestius speeded up his retreat by discarding all unnecessary supplies and killing all beasts of burden except those needed to carry missiles and engines of war. Even so, he was almost annihilated by his Jewish pursuers and only escaped by a forced march and an ignominious flight under the cover of night. The Romans and their allies lost 5,300 foot soldiers and 480 cavalry. Cestius sent a report of the disaster to Nero, laying the responsibility for the war upon Florus, hoping in this way to divert the blame for the disaster from himself.

Returning to Jerusalem from their victory over Cestius, the triumphant Jews, partly by force, partly by persuasion, brought over to their side such pro-Romans as still remained, and began organizing for all-out war. Full authority over the city's affairs was given to Joseph, son of Gorion, and to Ananus, the High Priest with special responsibility for raising the height of the walls. Eleazar, son of Simon, who had taken possession of all the booty, the war supplies, and the treasure captured from the defeated Roman governor, Cestius, was made commander. Other generals were selected: for Idumaea, Jericho, Peraea, and the provinces of Thamnia, Gophna, and Acrabetta. And I, Josephus, son of Matthias, was given command over the two Galilees, with the addition of Gamala, the strongest city in that region.

Each of these generals carried out his assigned task to the best of his ability. As for myself, on my arrival in Galilee, I made it my first care to win the goodwill of the people. I knew that Galilee would bear the brunt of the Romans' opening assault, so I fortified the most defensible positions, namely, Jotapata, Bersabe, Japhna, Tarichaeae, and Tiberias, among others. I raised an army of upwards of 100,000 young men, all of whom I equipped with old weapons which I managed to get together. I organized this army on Roman lines and increased the number of junior officers. I created ranks for the soldiers and appointed over them commanders of tens, called decurions, and of hundreds, called centurions. Over them tribunes and generals were in command. Above all I trained them for war by stressing the discipline maintained by the Romans, who, by their vigor and bravery, had become masters of almost the whole world.

I had now mustered an army, ready for action, of 60,000 infantry, and 350 cavalry, besides some 4,500 professional fighters, in whom I had the most confidence. I also had a bodyguard of 600 hand-picked men. These troops, except for the mercenaries, were maintained by the towns, which sent out only half of their conscripts at any one time, while keeping back the remainder to provide the necessary supplies.

While I was thus directing affairs in Galilee, there appeared on the scene a schemer from the city of Gischala, who was named John, son of Levi. He was unscrupulous and crafty, a liar, cruel, and greedy. He started out as a poor man, all alone, but soon collected a band of four hundred men, all bold, all physically formidable and all skillful fighters, with whose help he plundered much of Galilee. He was ambitious to be a general and maybe even more, but he was hindered by his lack of money. John saw that at first I was pleased by his show of energy. He persuaded me to entrust him with the rebuilding of the walls of Gischala, an undertaking in which he made himself wealthy at the expense of the well-to-do citizens of his native town. John hoped to get rid of me and become general in Galilee himself. He ordered his gang to stir up more and more disturbances and to spread lawlessness and anarchy. He spread slanderous rumors on all sides that I intended to betray the country to the Romans.

About this time some young men robbed a caravan of rich vestments, a quantity of silver goblets, and six hundred pieces of gold, all belonging to King Agrippa and his sister, Berenice. These young men could not dispose of the booty secretly so they turned it over to me while I was in the city of Tarichaeae. I was furious at the outrage to the king's servants and took the stolen goods and put them into the hands of a trusted citizen of the town for safekeeping, intending to return them to their legitimate owners as soon as I could. This action brought me into the greatest danger. The plunderers, suspecting my plan, scurried about the villages at night and denounced me as a traitor. A mob, whipped up by John of Gischala, collected in Tarichaeae at dawn and clamored for my head. My bodyguards fled while I was still asleep. I awoke only when my enemies were about to burn down my house over my head. Undaunted, I rushed out with my clothing torn and ashes sprinkled on my head, my hands behind my back and my sword dangling from my neck. My purpose was to trick my angry enemies by seeming to be ready to make a full confession. When I finally managed to speak, I addressed the crowd and told the people that, far from intending to return the treasures or to appropriate them for myself, my plan was to use them to build the walls for the city of Tarichaeae, whose ramparts had not been reconstructed because of lack of funds. At these words, the people of Tarichaeae applauded, while those from other places argued and threatened. The opposing sides left me alone and turned to quarreling with themselves. I spoke up once again promising to fortify all other cities with funds that would be forthcoming if the people would join against the common enemy instead of against me.

On another occasion, John tried to foment a revolt against me in the city of Tiberias and almost succeeded in assassinating me when I rushed to the city to put down the plot and stood speaking to the people, but I escaped, with two of my guards, by jumping from a mound, nine feet high, into a boat that was moored in the lake, the Sea of Galilee. Now I was sure of John's plots against me. I took action against his followers and broke up their ranks by threatening to seize their property and their families if they did not abandon their scheming leader. Three thousand of John's followers threw down their arms and came over to my side. The city of Tiberias rose up in revolt a second time and now turned to King Agrippa and appealed for help against me. The gates of the city were barred against me and I had to act quickly. The following day was the Sabbath, when I could not move. The main body of my troops was out in search of food. I resorted to a stratagem, using 230 boats which were on the lake, manning each one with no more than four sailors. I myself made full speed for Tiberias and fooled the people into surrendering without a fight. On that occasion, with empty ships far out in the water so that they could not be seen clearly, and with only seven armed guards, I overcame the entire population and kept Tiberias under control.

After all these disturbances in Galilee were quelled and the internal strife ended, the Jews turned to preparations for the war with the Romans. In Jerusalem, repairs went forward on all the walls. Engines of war were collected. In all quarters of the city, missiles and suits of armor were being forged. Masses of young men were being trained in haphazard fashion, the whole resulting in one huge scene of tumult and confusion, overcast with a feeling of doom and destruction.

At this time, too, another large band of revolutionaries appeared on the scene under the command of a new ambitious rebel chieftain, Simon, son of Gioras, who not only plundered and mistreated the wealthy but, from the beginning, showed signs of his later arrogance. The leaders in Jerusalem sent an army out against Simon, but he refused to do battle. Instead he retired with his followers to the mountain fortress of Masada, where he fortified himself and remained for some time.

II

Vespasian
CAPITOLINE MUSEUM,
ROME. ANDERSON

The news of the revolt in Judea filled Emperor Nero with alarm. Nero needed a general capable of putting down the Jewish rebels and of preventing the spread of unrest to neighboring lands, which were already beginning to smolder. He decided on Vespasian, a veteran soldier, who had grown gray in the service of Rome. Vespasian had pacified the Germans and had added Britain to the Roman Empire for the glory of Nero's stepfather, Claudius.

Nero sent Vespasian as general to take command of the armies in Syria. Immediately the general sent his son, Titus, to Alexandria to bring up the Fifteenth Legion from that city. He himself crossed the Hellespont and proceeded by land to Antioch, capital of Syria. Antioch was a city of great size and wealth, unqestionably the third in importance among the cities of the Empire, after Rome and Alexandria. Here Vespasian found Agrippa waiting with all his own troops. Vespasian at

Spring, 67 A.D.

The Romans used cavalry for swift attacks and pursuits.
SARCOPHAGUS OF ST. HELENA.
VATICAN MUSEUM
ANDERSON

once pushed on into Galilee, where he was met by the citizens of the city of Sepphoris, who had already shown that they had no intention of fighting the Romans. Sepphoris had admitted a Roman garrison; now it welcomed the commander-in-chief. Vespasian made the city the base for a large force of cavalry and infantry because of its strong, strategic position inside the enemy's territory. The Romans made constant forays from their fortified positions and overran the surrounding country, creating serious difficulties for me and my men. If, as the Jewish commander, I kept my men behind the fortifications of our own cities, the Romans were free to ravage the district. If we ventured out, the Romans engaged us and beat us back. I, Josephus, tried a direct assault on Sepphoris to stop the Romans, but I had fortified the city myself so strongly that the attack was unsuccessful.

Titus, meanwhile, came up with the Fifteenth Legion from Egypt and joined his father, who had with him the Fifth and Tenth. The total strength of the Roman forces, including the contingents supplied by the subject kings, amounted to sixty thousand, even without the vast numbers of servants who should also be counted as combatants since they were trained militarily alongside their masters. Vespasian drew up his army for the march in the customary Roman order. Lightly armed auxiliary troops and archers were sent out as advance parties to repel any sudden enemy attacks and to scout woodlands that might conceal any surprise traps. Next came a contingent of heavily armed Roman soldiers, infantry and cavalry. These were followed by a detachment from each hundred, carrying the necessary tools to mark out the campsites. After them came workers and engineers to straighten out any bends in the road, to level rough surfaces, and to cut down obstructing woods. Behind these came the baggage of the commander and his generals, protected by a strong mounted escort. Vespasian followed with the elite of the infantry and cavalry and his own guard of lancers. Next came the cavalry units, followed by the mules carrying the siege towers, the battering rams, and the other war machines. Then came commanders and officers, followed by the battle standards with the Roman eagle, which are always with every legion, and also the trumpeters. Behind them came the main body, shoulder to shoulder, marching as a solid column, six abreast. Behind the infantry came the servants and auxiliaries and last of all, for security, a rear guard composed of light and heavy infantry and a strong body of cavalry.

With his whole army in this order, Vespasian had reached the frontiers of Galilee. Here he paused and made a show of his forces to inspire terror in the hearts of his foes. In this he succeeded somewhat, for many of the troops under my command melted away without even a skirmish. I, Josephus, saw that my

A model of a Roman soldier carrying a typical battle standard.
ALINARI

May–June, 67 A.D.

OPPOSITE:
The Roman army building earthworks and platforms against the walls of a fortified city.
COLUMN OF TRAJAN, ROME.
GERMAN ARCHAEOLOGICAL INSTITUTE

strength was too reduced to risk an engagement. The morale of my men had collapsed, and I began to fear the final outcome of the war. For the moment, to avoid any pitched battle, I withdrew to Tiberias with the remnants of my troops. I thereupon notified the authorities in Jerusalem of the exact situation, neither exaggerating the strength of the Roman enemy, nor underrating it. I suggested that if the leaders in Jerusalem were intending to sue for terms with the Romans that they do so without delay. But, if they were determined to fight the war, they were requested to send adequate forces capable of coping with the Romans.

Vespasian, on the other hand, turned now on Jotapata, which he heard was a main base for the Jews. Jotapata was a strong bastion, built on a steep cliff, protected on three sides by deep ravines. Only on the north side, where the town straggled up the spur of a mountain, could it be approached. I hurried from Tiberias and slipped into Jotapata, my arrival being greeted with great enthusiasm by the Jewish defenders. Vespasian considered the news of my presence a stroke of very good fortune, for he believed that one of his chief opponents had deliberately walked into a trap. He ordered the town surrounded so tightly that no one could go in or out.

The siege of Jotapata lasted for forty-seven days. The defenders, made bold by despair, tried sally after sally against the Roman ranks encircling the city. The Romans, with military skill and experience, absorbed the shocks and then rallied, driving the attackers back behind the city's walls. Vespasian began throwing up earthworks. The besieged countered with great

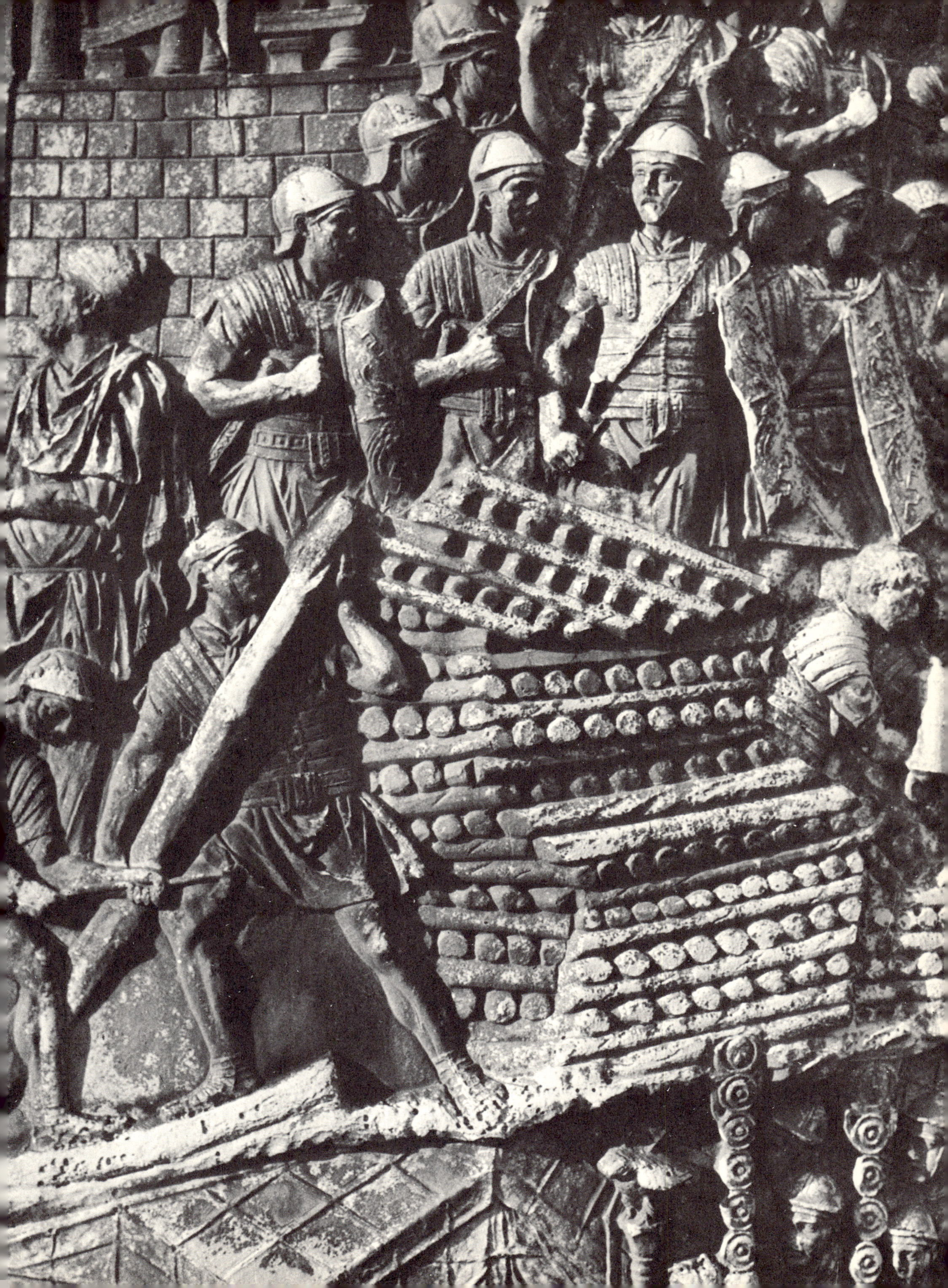

OPPOSITE:
Submission of prisoners to a Roman emperor, exemplified in a bas relief of Marcus Aurelius (161–180 A.D.).
ARCH OF CONSTANTINE, ROME.
ALINARI ART REFERENCE BUREAU

June–July, 67 A.D.

boulders which they hurled down on the Romans. I summoned all the town's stonemasons and, protected by ingenious shields of ox hides, they raised the walls to a height of thirty feet. Vespasian then decided to starve the city into submission, knowing how meager a water supply was available. However, I had rationed water from the very outset, and, to deceive the Romans, I ordered dripping garments to be hung all around the battlements, as though water was so plentiful that we could afford to waste it. Then Vespasian gave up hope of starving the city and returned to the attack. But I recognized that the city could not hold out for long and I began to plan a diversion. I would go for help, I told the people, and come back to the aid of the town. But the defenders of the Jotapata pleaded with me not to desert them. The Romans then brought up their mightiest battering ram and the walls of the city soon began to shake. We fought back with every trick we could devise, such as lowering sacks filled with chaff in front of the battering ram so that they absorbed the shock of the blows like a cushion. But the Romans reacted quickly too and attached sharp scythes to the ends of long poles and so cut down the hanging sacks. The battle continued in this manner, back and forth, attack and counterattack. Vespasian himself was wounded by an arrow which struck the sole of his foot. The Roman onslaught grew in fierceness. Hand-to-hand fighting ensued. The Romans formed a solid roof of shields and pushed the Jewish defenders up to the wall. I ordered boiling oil poured on these close-locked shields and broke up the formation. We poured slippery herbs on the Roman bridges and gangways, and the troops lost footing

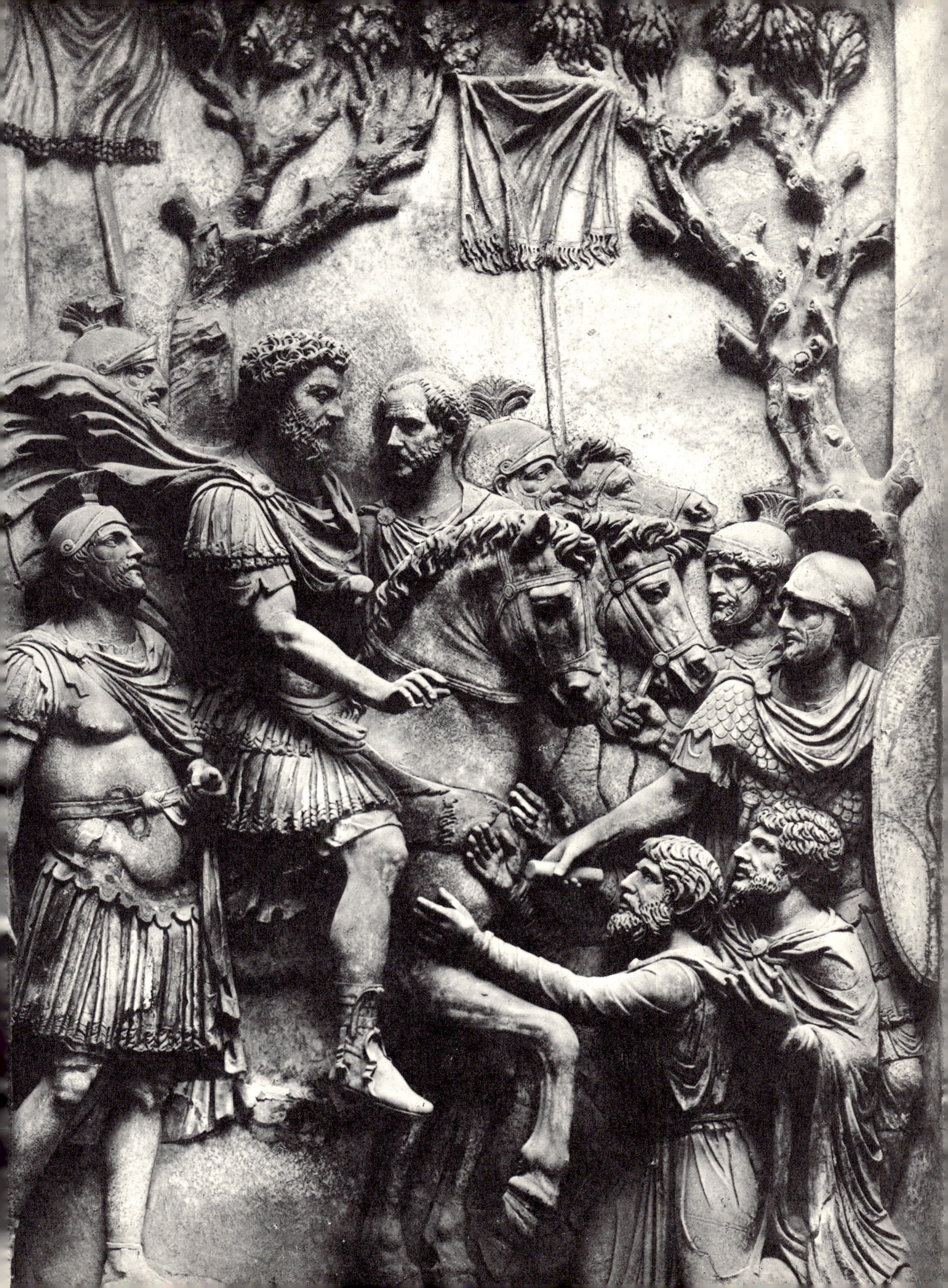

and were crushed. On the forty-seventh day of the siege, the Roman earthworks reached higher than the city walls. That night a suprise attack on the weary sentries succeeded.

By the time it was daylight, the Roman enemy was ranging through the heart of the town. Jotapata was taken. The Romans massacred everyone they found. They searched hiding places, vaults, and caverns, sparing no one except twelve hundred women and children who were taken prisoner. The total number killed was computed at forty thousand. Vespasian ordered the city to be razed and all of its fortifications burned. Thus fell Jotapata in the thirteenth year of Nero's rule.

July, 67 A.D.

I, Josephus, however, had managed to find a hiding place in a deep cave, along with forty other important persons of the city. We had sufficient supplies for a considerable time. All day long I stayed hidden in the cave, but at night I ventured forth looking for a way to escape. The Romans searched the city for me with great care, but until the third day they found no trace of us. Then the secret of my hiding place was betrayed by a woman prisoner, and Vespasian sent officers to offer me a safe conduct. Vespasian dispatched another messenger, a tribune, Nicanor by name, who was an old friend of mine, to help in persuading me that my fight had won admiration for me not hatred. I was assured that Vespasian wanted to rescue me not trap me. While Nicanor was thus urging his proposals, some soldiers tried to smoke us out by setting fires in the cave. Suddenly there came to my mind the many dreams I had had, in which God had foretold me of the impending disaster of the Jews and of the fortunate prospects ahead for the Roman emperors. I was a priest myself, and a descendant of a long line of priests, an interpreter of dreams, and skilled in reading the hidden meanings in the Sacred Writings.

Recalling these dreadful dreams, I turned my face to God in silent prayer: "Since it pleases Thee, who didst create the Jewish nation, to visit Thy wrath now on it; since all good fortune has gone over to the side of the Romans; and since Thou chose my spirit to make known things that are still to come, I willingly surrender to the Romans, but I take Thee to witness that I go, not as a traitor, but as Thy servant."

But, to my consternation, the Jews who shared my hiding place crowded around me and threatened to kill me if I made a move to surrender to Nicanor and the Romans. They shouted: "Surely the shame would cry out to heaven for such a deed, defying our God-given spirit which despises death! Are you so fearful for your life, Josephus, that you would rather live a slave? How quickly you have forgotten your own words! How many have you inspired to lay down their lives for liberty! False, absolutely false, was your reputation for courage and cleverness!"

My companions urged me to die at my own hands, as befitted a general of the Jews, rather than as a traitor at the hands of the Romans. They pointed their swords at me and threatened to run me through. I tried to dissuade them from mass suicide, but they would not listen. They rushed at me, but I stood them off, making them still respect me as their commander. Thinking quickly, I proposed a lottery to decide the order of death. By luck or by God's providence, I was left alone with just one other, whom I persuaded to remain alive. Thus I survived the war, the Romans, and my own compatriots.

I was brought into Vespasian's presence, where the conquering Romans flocked to see me, some exulting at my downfall, some threatening, some calling for my instant death. Titus, however, was moved by my youth and courage. His pleading with his father was the main influence in saving my life. Thereupon Vespasian ordered me to be guarded with utmost care, intending to send me to Rome to Nero. Learning of this, I asked for an interview with Vespasian, which he granted. Vespasian was alone with his son, Titus, when I was brought in. I told the Roman commander that I was not an ordinary prisoner of war but a messenger of great destinies, sent by God. Otherwise, I assured him, I would have known how to die as becomes a general. Why send me to Nero, I asked Vespasian, when soon Vespasian himself would be the Emperor of Rome and his son, too. At first Vespasian was suspicious about my suggestions, but he soon became convinced of my ability to foresee the future. So though he did not undo my bonds, Vespasian sent me gifts of clothing and other comforts and ordered me treated with kindness and solicitude.

After the fall of Jotapata, Vespasian withdrew his troops to Caesarea to rest. At this time other disturbances broke out in Joppa, a base of a fleet of pirate ships that preyed on the seaborne commerce along the coasts of Syria and Phoenicia. Vespasian sent out a contingent to put down these pirates, who fled to their ships. A sudden storm blew up and destroyed the entire fleet. Four thousand and two hundred bodies were washed up on the beaches. The Romans leveled the town to the ground.

A Roman ship transporting troops.
VATICAN MUSEUM. ANDERSON

When the news of the fall of Jotapata reached Jerusalem, it was received at first with general disbelief. The disaster was so great as to defy comprehension, besides which not a single eyewitness appeared to confirm any of the reports. Not a man had escaped to tell the tragic tale. I was reported to have fallen when the city fell, which filled Jerusalem with deep grief. For thirty days the mournful lamentations over my reported death never ceased in the city, and many of the mourners hired flute-players to accompany their funeral dirges. But when time revealed the true state of affairs, that my death was untrue and that I was alive and in Roman hands, being treated with no little consideration and respect, Jerusalem exploded in wrath against me, as loud as the previous expressions of affection when I was believed to be dead. Some abused me as a coward, others

65

Titus

as a traitor, and throughout the city, curses were heaped upon my head.

Vespasian, in the meanwhile, had gone to visit Agrippa's kingdom, journeying from Caesarea-on-the-sea to the other Caesarea, called Caesarea-Philippi. There he rested his troops for twenty days. While he was there, word came of uprisings in Tiberias and in Tarichaeae, both cities inside the boundaries of Agrippa's kingdom. Vespasian determined to march against the rebels, as much to repay Agrippa's hospitality as to maintain his own resolve to crush Jewish opposition wherever it arose. There were two camps in Tiberias: the elders and more respected citizens favored Rome, the others were openly defiant. The insurgents, after making a small show of resistance towards the Romans, retreated to Tarichaeae, and Vespasian occupied Tiberias without opposition. As a favor to Agrippa, he did not sack the city. Meanwhile all the revolutionaries were flocking towards Tarichaeae, hoping to find protection in the strength of the city and its nearness to the Sea of Galilee. Like Tiberias, the city was built at the foot of the hills. In fact I had completely surrounded it with solid walls on every side except the one washed by the lake. The main body of the Jews assembled on the plain outside the town. Vespasian sent ahead his son, Titus, with six hundred handpicked cavalry. Titus found himself heavily outnumbered and sent for reinforcements.

While waiting, Titus found a spot where he could be heard by his troops and he addressed them as follows: "Romans, bear in mind who you are and whom we have to fight. Up to now no nation in the world has succeeded in escaping our power, even though the Jews, to give them their due, have so far staunchly refused to accept defeat. But the Jews, however dauntless and reckless of life they may be, are yet undisciplined and unskilled in war. They should be called a rabble, not an army. Consider that you will be in full armor, up against men with scarcely any armor. You are cavalry against infantry. You have seasoned leaders, they have none. The Jews are carrying on by courage, nerve, and despair, emotions which are very inspiring in the flush of success. But they evaporate at the slightest reversal of fortune. We, on the other hand, have valor, discipline, and a heroism which endures to the very last. In addition, you will be fighting for a nobler cause than the Jews, even though they face the war for liberty and country. What higher motive could there be for us than glory and the determination, after having conquered the world, not to let the Jews be regarded as a match for us! For myself, I believe that all of us are on trial, my father, myself, and all of you. It will be seen whether my father still deserves his reputation, whether I am worthy to be his son, and you to be my soldiers."

Titus then led the charge, spurring his horse against the enemy. The Jews, though taken aback by the fury and discipline of the attack, for a while sustained the Roman charges. But, pierced by the lances and overthrown by the rush of the horses, many fell and were trampled underfoot. The Jews retreated headlong back into the town, despite Titus' efforts to head them off and cut them down. Inside the city, sharp fighting broke out between the native inhabitants of Tarichaeae who disapproved of the war and the desperate newcomers who had been routed by the Romans. Titus, seeing his opportunity, leapt onto his horse, led his troops to the lake, rode through the water and charged, the first to enter the town. There was a great slaughter, with no distinction between the defiant rebels and the peaceful residents. At length, Titus called a halt to the massacre. Several thousands of the Jews tried to escape in ships across the Sea of Galilee, but the Romans pursued them on a flotilla of rafts. A fierce naval battle ensued and the Jewish fleet was destroyed. Many of the Jews were speared in the water; many reached the shore where they were slain by the Romans. The whole lake was red with blood and covered with corpses, for not a man who had fled escaped.

After the battle, Vespasian separated the city's peaceful population from the hordes of others who had fought the Romans and with the promise of a safe conduct sent the troublemaking interlopers to Tiberias. There he went back on his word and herded them into the stadium of the city, where he ordered the execution of the old and unuseful, numbering twelve hundred. Of the younger persons, he selected six thousand healthy individuals and sent them to Nero. The rest of the mass of prisoners, with the exception of some whom he presented to Agrippa, he sold into slavery. They numbered 30,400. In turn, Agrippa also sold the ones that had been given to him.

III

After the Roman success at Tarichaeae, most Galileans, even those who had continued their rebellion after the fall of Jotapata, surrendered. The Romans received the submission of all fortresses and towns except Gischala and Gamala, a city situated on the other side of the Sea of Galilee, and the force on Mt. Tabor. Gamala refused to surrender, relying confidently on the natural strength of its position on the hump of a rugged spur, descending from a lofty mountain. The ridge resembled the back of a camel, which in the native language is a "gamal," hence the name of the city. Vespasian broke his camp at Tiberias and marched on Gamala. He set up outposts wherever he could and occupied in force the mountain overhanging the city. He ordered the construction of earthworks, which were rapidly completed, and the engines of war brought into position. The battering rams went to work at three different quarters. Soon the Romans broke through the wall and poured through the

Roman artillery: a model of a catapult, which could hurl heavy boulders with great force.

breach with loud trumpet blasts, clash of arms, and battle cries.

Pursuing the enemy to the higher parts of the town, the Romans suddenly found themselves in narrow quarters, unable to push back their adversaries or to fall back through the ranks of their own comrades who were pressing from behind. Many Romans were forced to climb on to the roofs of the enemy houses, which in places reached close to the sloping ground. Soon these roofs caved in, one house collapsing and bringing down with it other houses built on the lower slopes beneath. Many of the Romans were buried in these ruins and many died of suffocation from the dust. Even Vespasian himself found himself in personal peril, from which he escaped only by a show of great valor.

To take the minds of the troops off this setback, Vespasian sent six hundred horsemen on a diversionary attack on the defenders of Mt. Tabor, who were quickly reduced to submission. Titus, who had been away during the first assault on Gamala, was outraged by the reverses which the Romans had suffered. He selected two hundred cavalry and a body of infantry and moved into the city. The defenders snatched up their children and fled to the higher sections of the town. Vespasian now brought up his main force which was met with a rain of missiles and of all kinds of rocks which were rolled down upon them from above. However, a fierce storm arose, blowing full into the faces of the defenders, which hurled against them the full force of the arrows of the Romans, while blunting and deflecting their own. The gale made it impossible for the defenders to keep firm footholds on the rugged cliffs. On top of it all, the storm veiled the approach of the Roman attackers. Many, in despair, plunged headlong, together with their wives and children, into the yawning ravines which had been dug around the fortified heights.

Only Gischala, a small town, now remained unsubdued in all of Galilee. Gischala was the home mainly of farmers, who would probably have surrendered to the Romans. But egged on by my enemy, John, son of Levi, a man of monumental cunning and ambition, the rebellious spirits in the town persuaded the rest of the people to defy the attackers. Against these rebels, Vespasian sent Titus and a contingent of a thousand cavalrymen. Titus could have taken the town easily by assault, but, knowing it would lead to massacre, he urged the inhabitants to capitulate. John of Gischala replied to Titus from the walls of the city, saying that he agreed to the proposals and would see to it that they were obeyed. But, he said, Titus must allow them

Judea and surrounding districts at the time of the Roman-Jewish War

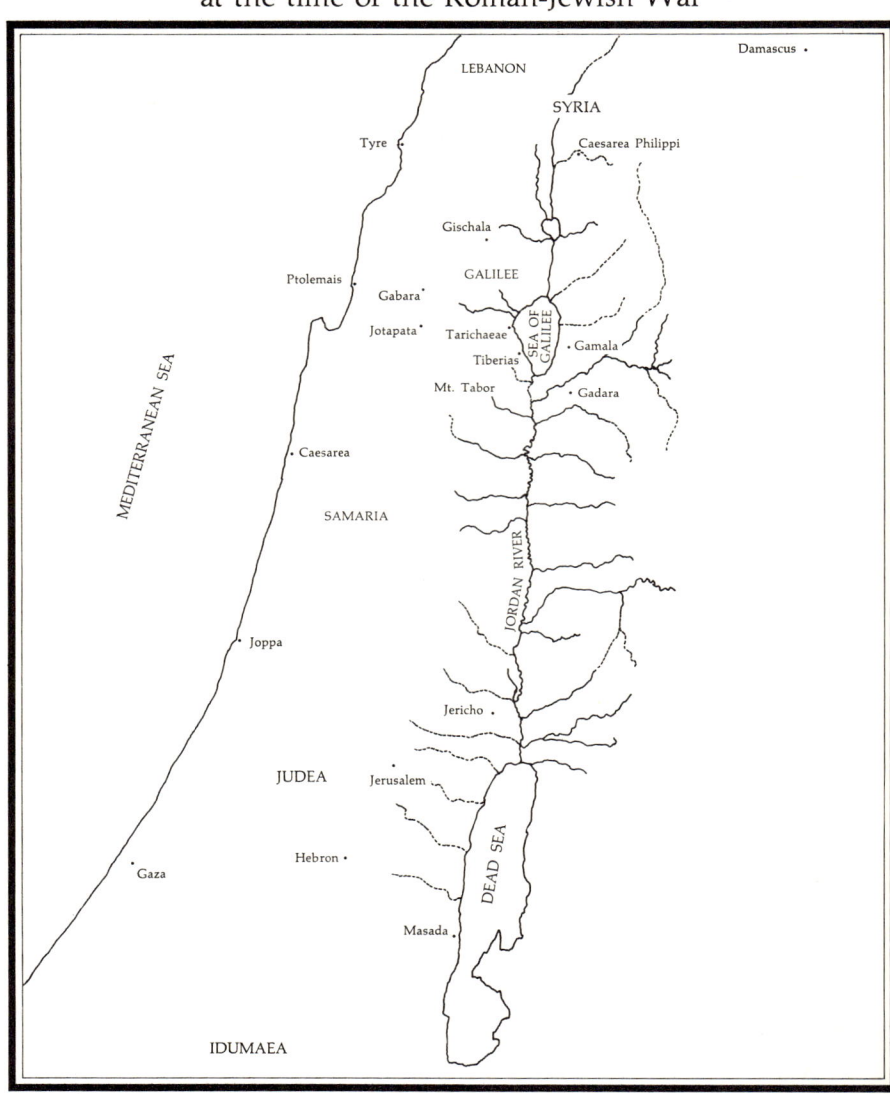

that day, it being the seventh day of the week, since it was forbidden by Jewish law either to wage war or to conclude a treaty of peace on the Sabbath. Titus agreed. That night, John of Gischala and his followers stealthily crept out of the town and fled headlong for Jerusalem. Early the next day, Titus entered the town and learned of John's escape. Titus at once sent a squadron of cavalry in pursuit but John could not be overtaken. With the fall of Gischala, all of Galilee was now subdued. The campaign had provided the Romans with tough training for the assault against Jerusalem, which was now impending.

Reaching Jerusalem safely, John immediately spread stories ridiculing the Romans, calling them weak and praising the power of the Jews. Even if the Romans had wings, he told everyone, they could never get over the walls of Jerusalem, seeing how much difficulty they had met with in Galilee and how they had worn out their war engines against simple village walls. By such methods most of the young people of Jerusalem were seduced into his service and their war spirit inflamed. But the older and more sober men already foresaw the future and mourned for the city as if it had already met its doom. Such was the confusion in Jerusalem, but even before open conflict appeared in the city, civil war broke out in the countryside. The war parties and the peace parties fought fiercely with one another. The bitter struggle destroyed friendships and families. But finally the militant party, because of its youthfulness and boldness, won the upper hand over the old and prudent.

Bands of brigands roamed the countryside, pillaging their neighbors. In the end, tired of robbing poor villagers, the brigand chiefs joined forces and converged on poor Jerusalem—a city under no strong commanding officer, and one which, by ancient custom, admitted all of Jewish blood without question. This circumstance, even if there had been no civil war, eventually would have wrecked the city, for food supplies which might have been enough for the defenders were being squandered on a useless and idle mob. These brigands now visited their outrages on the city, openly, in broad daylight. First they arrested some of the most eminent citizens and, charging them with treason, arbitrarily executed them. These outlaws rose to such heights of arrogance as to take over the right to elect the high priest, denying the claims of the families from whom the high priests had always been drawn. With unholy feet they even invaded the Holy Sanctuary. Thus these bandits, now calling themselves Zealots, converted the Temple of God into a fortress and the Holy Place into the main headquarters of their tyranny.

One of the chief old priests, named Ananus, a man of reason and sanity, raised the populace against the Zealots, and fierce fighting broke out in the streets. The people of Jerusalem, now roused to fury, poured forth in growing numbers and headed towards the Temple. There followed barrages of stones from both sides, not only in front of the Temple but all over the city. After that came a long-range combat with spears and javelins. The Zealots could not stand up under the pressure of so many angry people and withdrew into the Temple, fleeing into the inner court and barring the gates behind them. The priest, Ananus, selected a force of six thousand armed men, whom he posted to guard the great doorways. At this point, John of

Gischala pretended to side with Ananus and the people, but each night he revealed all their plans and secrets to the Zealots. So for a long time Jerusalem kept warring with itself.

The Zealots then called for help upon the Idumaeans, falsely charging Ananus with being in league with the Romans. The Idumaeans immediately responded and came rushing to the city. Even more pillage, murder, and bloodshed became the order of the day. The Idumaeans captured Ananus, the high priest, and put him to death, which I should not be wrong in saying was the beginning of the end of the city, the downfall of its walls and the ruin of the Jewish state. Now the Zealots and the Idumaeans butchered the people as though they were a herd of unclean animals. They arrested young men of good families and threw them into prison, dangling life or death before them in the hopes of winning them over. Not one, however, could be seduced by these overtures, all preferring to die rather than side with such villains. Thus twelve thousand of the youthful nobility perished.

The Roman generals, considering this dissension in the enemy ranks as a gift of the gods, were all eager to march against Jerusalem and urged Vespasian, their commander-in-chief, to move without delay. Vespasian, however, did not agree. If he immediately attacked the city, he said, the effect would be to reunite the Jews; whereas if he waited, they would destroy themselves and there would be fewer enemies to do battle with. Consequently, while the Jews were dying by their own hands and suffering from that worst of all calamities—civil war—the Romans could not do better than to sit as distant spectators, leaving to the Jews their own destruction. The Roman generals bowed to Vespasian's counsel.

But now John of Gischala felt ready to make a bid for supreme power over Jerusalem. He built up his own following of reckless hotheads and broke away from his alliance with the other Zealots. At this time, too, the *sicarii*, who had entrenched themselves on the fortified mound of Masada, again began marauding expeditions against many of the villages around the fortress.

Vespasian was kept abreast of everything that was happening by spies and informers who managed to flee to the Romans. Deciding that the time to move had come, Vespasian broke camp with the apparent aim of taking Jerusalem. But first it was necessary to clean up any outstanding areas of resistance so that no threat to his campaign would be left to hinder him. First he marched on Gadara, the capital of the province of Peraea and a city of some strength. The leading men of the city sent an embassy to the Romans offering to capitulate. When the war party in the city learned of this, as the Roman legions approached, the rebellious elements were infuriated and vented their anger on the man, who by rank and family was the first man of the town. They slew him and then fled. The Gadarenes, as the Roman army appeared, pulled down their own walls.

Vespasian sent a large body of mounted men and foot soldiers in pursuit of those who had fled from Gadara. There were many skirmishes and much bloodshed, with the Jews being cut to pieces despite their great courage and daring. As a result, the entire area was thrown into panic. Everyone began running

Galba

for Jericho, that being the one remaining city strong enough to hold out some hope of safety. But the Romans drove on relentlessly and overtook them and pushed them up against the River Jordan, where they were blocked by the stream that was swollen by rain and impassable. Fifteen thousand perished at the hands of the Romans. The number of those who were driven to fling themselves into the Jordan could not be reckoned. The river was choked with the dead. Even the Dead Sea was filled with bodies, masses of which were carried down into it by the Jordan River. Thus the whole of the district of Paraea either surrendered or was subdued.

Meanwhile, tidings reached Vespasian of the revolt in faraway Gaul, at the other end of the Roman Empire. The news stimulated him to push on with the Jewish war more vigorously, for he already foresaw the impending civil strife facing Rome and the perils piling up for the Empire as a whole. He hoped that an early pacification in the East would help allay the anxiety of Rome. So at the approach of spring he marched southward from Caesarea and subdued the countryside of Judea and Idumaea, putting upwards of ten thousand of the inhabitants to death and making prisoners of over a thousand. He then marched on Jericho, which was found practically deserted. He established a camp there with a view to surrounding Jerusalem from every side. He established another camp at Adida, with the the same plan in mind, placing in each a garrison of both Roman soldiers and auxiliaries. Then he sent a squadron of cavalry and a considerable body of infantry against the city of Gerasa, which was captured by assault and burned to the ground.

Otho.

Vespasian now had all escape from Jerusalem cut off.

Vespasian had returned to Caesarea and was preparing to advance in full strength upon Jerusalem itself, when the news reached him that Nero had been slain, after ruling for over thirteen years. I do not propose to tell any more of the war in Gaul nor of its outcome, nor of Galba's call to the throne and how he was assassinated in the Forum in Rome, nor of Otho, who then was made emperor. Nor will I recount Otho's battles with the generals of Vitellius and his downfall, nor of the bloody fighting around Rome. Vespasian, when the news first came, postponed his expedition against Jerusalem, anxiously waiting to see who would inherit the Empire after Nero's death. When he heard that Galba was enthroned, he still hesitated, waiting for further instructions from him concerning the war. But he did send his son, Titus, to the new Emperor to salute him and to receive his orders regarding the war against the Jews. King Agrippa also set sail with Titus on the same errand. However, before they reached their destination, Galba was assassinated after a reign of seven months and as many days and was succeeded by Otho, his rival. Agrippa decided to keep on going to Rome, undeterred by this change of affairs. But Titus, as though by divine inspiration, sailed back to Syria and rejoined his father. The two, with the Roman Empire itself reeling, held back from any further campaigns in Judea. They were in great anxiety about Rome.

But another war was now hanging over Jerusalem. There was that rebel chief, Simon, son of Gioras, who had withdrawn with his men to Masada. Simon was a youth, less cunning than

John of Gischala, but far superior to him in physical strength and courage. Simon quit Masada and gathered around him increasing numbers of freed bondsmen and adventurers, who flocked to him from all sides. In the beginning he stayed in the hills for safety, but, as his following swelled into an army of more than serfs and brigands, he came down into the lowland country. Simon's followers now included many citizen recruits who were attracted by his strength and his successes.

The Zealots, worried by Simon's growing power, sallied forth from Jerusalem with their main forces, and a battle ensued. Simon drove the Zealots back with severe losses, but he did not yet feel confident enough to assault Jerusalem. He resolved therefore first to subdue the neighboring province of Idumaea. He marched with his army of twenty thousand men towards the frontiers of that territory. The chieftains of Idumaea mustered their best troops, numbering around 25,000, and met Simon at the border. A battle was fought that lasted all day, but neither victory nor defeat graced the field for either side. Later, by subterfuge, Simon took Idumaea without bloodshed. By another surprise attack he captured the little town of Hebron, where he won abundant booty and vast supplies of corn. According to the statements of its inhabitants, Hebron is a town older not only than any other in the country, but of even greater age than Memphis in Egypt. Its age is reckoned to be 2,300 years. They further relate that it was in Hebron that Abraham, the first patriarch of the Jews, made his home after his migration from Mesopotamia. It is said also that the descendants of Abraham went down from Hebron into Egypt.

Simon, son of Gioras, marched through the whole of Idumaea, wreaking destruction everywhere, for in addition to his troops, he had forty thousand followers. Like a forest stripped bare by locusts, so in the wake of Simon's army nothing remained but a desert. Some places they burned, others they razed to the ground. All vegetation throughout the country vanished, either trodden under foot or consumed. The Zealots, alarmed at Simon's progress, were afraid to meet him in open battle. Instead they set traps and ambushes, in one of which they captured Simon's wife and a large number of her attendants. Simon immediately marched to the walls of Jerusalem and demanded her release, threatening vengeance on every man, woman, and child behind the walls. These threats so terrified everyone that the Zealots sent him back his wife.

April 17, 69 A.D.

Sedition and civil war were not, however, confined to Judea. After holding the reins of government in Rome for three months and two days, Otho put an end to himself. His army went over to Vitellius, who now descended upon Rome with his legions. During this time, Vespasian moved out from Caesarea again and advanced against parts of Judea that had not yet been reduced to submission. He ascended into the hill country and subdued two provinces, called Gophna and Acrabetta. His legions laid waste to the territory known as upper Idumaea and advanced on Hebron, which, as I have said, is in the hill country not far from Jerusalem. The Romans took the approaches to the ancient city by force, massacred all whom they found, young and old, and burned down the town. Every fortress was now conquered except Herodium, Masada, and

Machaerus, which were held by brigands. Jerusalem was now the one objective before the Romans.

Simon, meanwhile, spent some time rampaging through Idumaea, forcing great numbers to take refuge in Jerusalem. Soon he, too, headed for the Holy City. Inside the walls, the Zealots, led by John, were looting the houses of the wealthy, murdering, carousing, and torturing. But, if any tried to flee from John, he found an even bloodier reception from Simon, who had encamped around the walls. Every avenue of escape was thus cut off for anyone who might want to flee to the Romans. Just at this time, the Idumaeans, who were serving under John of Gischala, mutinied and drove him and the Zealot forces into the Temple. John mustered all his strength and prepared to lead an attack against the Idumaeans, who met with the chief priests of the city to take counsel on the way to meet the impending assault. But God, as later events proved, must have distorted their judgment. They worked out a scheme for their salvation, which turned out to be their destruction. In other words, in order to overthrow John, they decided to admit Simon into the city. With humble appeals, they set up a second tyrant over their heads. Simon haughtily consented to be their master. He entered Jerusalem and was acclaimed by the people as their savior and protector. But, once inside with his troops, he made it his sole concern to make sure of his own authority. Thus did Simon, son of Gioras, in the third year of the war, become master of Jerusalem, while John and the Zealots, locked in the Temple, began to despair. Simon mounted an attack on the Temple with the support of the citizens of Jerusalem, but

April–May, 69 A.D.

Vitellius.

his adversaries beat him off. Simon suffered heavy casualties both in dead and wounded, for the Zealots from their higher ground could maintain an easy, well-directed fire. Simon's attacks weakened, and most of his men lost heart. Still by his superiority in numbers he was able to keep control of his ground.

About this time, too, Rome was beset by heavy calamities. Vitellius arrived with his army and a vast motley crowd besides. They moved into Rome and turned the city into a camp of armed men, who eyed the wealth on every side and did not restrain their greed. Plunder and murder became common in Italy. Vespasian, having reduced all of the territory surrounding Jerusalem, returned to Caesarea, where he learned of the disturbances in Rome and that Vitellius had been named emperor. Vespasian was furious at this news, but he held himself in check. He could take no action because he was a long way from Rome and he knew that Fate could play him many a nasty trick before he could get there, it being the winter season and no time for traveling. However, his officers and men were not deterred by these considerations. They were already frankly discussing a revolution.

"Vespasian's claim to the Empire is better than that of Vitellius," they exclaimed indignantly. "Just as we are better soldiers than Vitellius' supporters. Surely, we have waged wars as arduous as the legions of Germany. We are in no way inferior in arms to the troops who brought back this tyrant from Germany."

Vespasian's legions inspired one another and began hailing him as emperor, urging him to step in and save the endangered

Empire. For a while Vespasian held back, quite forcibly setting forth all his reasons for refusing imperial honors. But, finally, failing to change the insistence of his men, Vespasian yielded to their call. At once he began to act as the Emperor. He set as his first objective the allegiance of Alexandria. He knew the supreme importance of Egypt as the granary of the Empire. Once it was in his hands, he would force Vitellius to surrender, since the populace of Rome would never permit itself to be starved. Vespasian also had his eyes on the two legions based at Alexandria. Accordingly, he at once sent dispatches to Tiberius Alexander, the governor of Egypt and Alexandria, informing him of the legion's wish to make Vespasian emperor and telling him that he wanted to enlist his cooperation and assistance. Tiberius Alexander read the letter in public and promptly called on his legions and the populace to take the oath of allegiance to Vespasian, to which they gladly responded.

All through the East, oaths of allegiance were being sworn to Vespasian. Everywhere fortune was favoring his wishes, and matters for the most part were growing more and more favorable. Vespasian thought back over all the divine providence which had assisted him to the throne and, among other omens, he recalled the words of his prisoner, Josephus, myself, who had ventured even in Nero's lifetime to hail him as emperor.

"It is disgraceful," he said, "that one who prophesied my rise should still be in chains."

Calling for me, he ordered me liberated.

Vespasian then made all necessary arrangements to appoint governors of all the provinces of Rome. Having done this he

Vespasian, far right, is greeted as Emperor of Rome by his son, Domitian (center).
CONSERVATORI MUSEUM, ROME
GERMAN ARCHAEOLOGICAL INSTITUTE

December 21, 69 A.D.

journeyed to Antioch. There, he decided it was urgent to hasten to Rome, where Vitellius was creating general disorder. Accordingly, he dispatched a substantial force of cavalry and infantry, which headed overland. At the same time, another legion loyal to Vespasian was rushing to Rome to do battle with Vitellius. This legion engaged some of the troops of Vitellius and cut them to pieces. It reached Rome where other troops of Vitellius gave battle in three different quarters of the city, but all perished to a man. Vitellius staggered out of the palace, drunk, knowing that his end had come, and was dragged through the mob and butchered. He had reigned eight months and five days. Vespasian's son, Domitian, was brought forward and recommended to the multitude to be the ruler until the arrival of his father. The people of Rome, freed at last from terror, acclaimed Vespasian emperor.

On reaching Alexandria, Vespasian was greeted by the good news from Rome. With the Empire now secured, Vespasian turned his thoughts to what remained in Judea. He was anxious to take ship for Rome as soon as the winter was over. So he gave over to his son, Titus, the task of crushing Jerusalem. Accordingly Titus proceeded by ship up the Nile with his army and then by land over the desert, crossing the frontier and arriving finally at Caesarea, the main base of his forces.

IV

While Titus was still in Alexandria helping his father secure the throne, it so happened that the civil strife in Jerusalem reached a fresh climax and became a three-sided fight, one of the parties having turned its arms against itself. This new development might be described as a faction bred within a faction, like a maddened beast driven by hunger to devour itself. For the first commander of Jewish forces in Jerusalem, Eleazar, son of Simon, the man who had forced the Zealots to withdraw into the Temple precincts, broke away from John of Gischala, taking with him several leaders, each of whom had a considerable following. This new faction took possession of the inner court of the Temple and planted its weapons above the Holy Gates. They were relatively few in numbers, but they had ample supplies. On the other hand, John's superiority in numbers was canceled by the disadvantage of his position below his new enemies. The two factions engaged in continual sallies, firing showers of missiles. On every side the Temple was soon defiled with bloodshed.

Then there was Simon, son of Gioras, who held the Upper City and a large part of the Lower City. He now attacked John's men more vigorously, seeing that they were also being assailed from above. John was thus between two fires. He stoutly repelled attacks from below with hand missiles, but he reserved his engines of war—his quick-firers, catapults, and stone-throwers—to check the hail of javelins from the Temple above. With these engines he beat off his assailants. At the same time, he also killed many innocent worshippers who came to offer sacrifices in the Holy Places. Many, from near and far, gathered round the Temple's far-famed altar, only to fall there themselves before their sacrifices, sprinkling with their own blood the altar so universally venerated. What misery to equal that, most wretched city, hast thou suffered at the hands of the Romans? Thou wert no longer God's place, nor couldst thou go on, after becoming the sepulchre for the bodies of thine own children! However, the laws of history compel one to restrain one's deepest emotions. This is not the place for personal lamentations, but for a narrative of the events.

Titus, having assembled part of his forces at Caesarea, ordered the remainder to join him at Jerusalem. He had the three legions which under his father had previously ravaged Judea, and the Twelfth which under Cestius had tasted defeat by the Jews. He also had new troops from Egypt, commanded by his loyal friend, Tiberius Alexander. Leading his army forward in orderly array, according to Roman usage, Titus advanced

Inside the wall separating the Upper from the Lower City (right), is a monument marking the site where the Tomb of David was believed to be at the time of the Second Temple. The tomb is now considered to be located in the original city of David, near the eastern wall. A semicircular theatre structure is in the upper right, with the outer wall of the Temple Mount in the background.

According to Josephus, the palace of Herod the Great in Jerusalem baffled all description. "Its magnificence and furnishings were unsurpassed." The palace was enclosed by a wall 45 feet high, studded with towers. Herod's palace was often under attack both from outside and from within the city. It was used by the Roman governors when they were in Jerusalem. A Roman garrison was dislodged from it and massacred by Jewish freedom fighters, who set fire to the palace. Cestius Gallus, Roman governor of Syria, mounted his unsuccessful attack on Jerusalem opposite Herod's palace. In the upper left, outside the palace walls, is the Upper Market.

The Royal Palace of the Hasmoneans was in the Upper City. In the background are the Upper Market and the wall enclosing Herod's palace. Berenice looked down from the roof of the Hasmonean palace as her brother, Agrippa II, tried unsuccessfully to dissuade the Jews from taking up arms against the Romans.

This view, looking over the cone-shaped domes of the Palace of the Hasmoneans toward the enclosure of the Temple Mount shows the western wall, which is still standing in Jerusalem, also called the Wailing Wall. To the left is the bridge connecting the Upper City with the Temple over the deep ravine which cuts through the city. Built by the Hasmoneans, the bridge is now called Wilson's Arch after its discoverer. Herod built a second bridge over the ravine (right), now called Robinson's Arch.

The Sanctuary (left), gleaming in the s[un]
towered over the Temple area, the city [of]
Jerusalem and the entire countryside. T[he]
restoration of the Second Temple was
begun by Herod who erected new
foundations, doubled the area it occupi[ed]
and erected columned halls and courty[ards.]
Within the Temple walls (foreground) [is]
the Women's Court. The Nicanor Gate
leads to the Sanctuary. In the backgrou[nd]
is the Fortress Antonia.

The Gates of Nicanor, leading to the
Sanctuary, were made of Corinthian
bronze and not gilt as were the other
Temple gates. According to tradition, t[he]
gates were miraculously saved when th[ey]
were being transported by Nicanor fro[m]
Alexandria during a storm. The facade [of]
the Sanctuary follows the rendition o[n a]
coin of the Second Revolt under Simon
bar-Kochba. Within the Sanctuary wa[s the]
Holy of Holies.

A model of ancient Jerusalem, representing the city during the period of the Second Temple, has been constructed to scale in the modern-day capital of the State of Israel. A reconstruction of the city as it was in the year 66 A.D.—just before the outbreak of the revolt against Rome—the model was planned and its buildings and monuments designed from evidence in archaeological and literary sources, among which the writings of Josephus figured prominently. The scale replica is built of the same materials used in the original construction of the city; marble, stone, wood, copper, and iron.

The model lends a startling immediacy to the bitter events that drowned the ancient city in blood. Imagination fills the miniature streets with people. Florus, last of the procurators, rampages through the city with his arrogant legionaries. Agrippa II, a king of Jewish blood, tries to calm the citizens' overflowing anger against their Roman ruler. The streets are crowded with dignified priests, lordly aristocrats, the hot-blooded freedom fighters. The daring "curved daggers" mingle with the crowds after a lightning attack. In the fall, the city is filled with pilgrims, who, seeing the Roman governor of Syria marching on Jerusalem, abandon their religious celebrations and turn the Roman advance into a rout. At the end of the year these same streets ring with the preparations for the revolt: the clanging forges making armor and missiles, the shouts of young men training to go to war.

At the northwest corner of Jerusalem's third wall stood the tower Psephinus, an eight-sided structure which kept watch over all Judea. It was 105 feet high and "afforded a view embracing both Arabia and the farthermost boundaries of Jewish territory as far as the sea." The advancing Roman legions, marching down from the north, were probably first sighted from this tower. Opposite the tower Psephinus, Titus established his first camp to begin the siege of Jerusalem.

In the old wall of Jerusalem, where it converges on the newer second and third walls, King Herod built a tower (left), which he named Hippicus, in memory of a friend. It was quadrangular in shape, with a reservoir to catch rainwater, and surmounted by a double-roofed chamber, totaling 120 feet in height. Herod built a second tower (upper right), which he named Phasael, after his brother. It contained sumptuous apartments and baths, and reached a total height of 135 feet. A third tower (background center), named for Herod's queen, Mariamme, "was far more luxurious and ornate as befitted a memorial to a woman." The towers protected the city from external attack but they also guarded against any threat from within against Herod's palace (which can be seen in the background behind them). In the right foreground is the tomb of John Hyrcanus, the High Priest. Titus began his assault on Jerusalem on the walls near this tomb, because here the fortifications were on lower ground.

Jerusalem was enclosed by three walls. The third, built by Agrippa I to protect the newer sections of the city, was the first to be breached by Titus, who razed it to the ground, destroying at the same time a large part of the sparsely built northern quarter of the city, which was new and expanding (foreground). After five days, Titus managed an entry through the second wall, visible in the center. This wall leads from the four-towered fortress of Antonia, guarding the Temple area (upper left), and turns south and east to the tower Hippicus (upper right) where it joins the first wall, the city's oldest, stretching from the Temple. Titus destroyed the northern section of the second wall. The massive fortress Antonia, named for Mark Antony by King Herod, was a central point in much of the struggle with Rome.

A. ERIS

Cramped and crowded, the Lower City was the home of Jerusalem's poor and the center of its commercial and industrial life. The Lower City was a stronghold of the freedom fighters in the revolt against Rome.

The Upper City was on the higher of the two hills of Jerusalem. It contained the homes of the wealthier inhabitants, and included the royal palaces, the Upper Market, and the palaces of the High Priests. In the foreground are the weaving and dyeing workshops, where priestly clothes were made. The Upper City was the last section of Jerusalem to fall to the Romans.

through Samaria to Gophna, previously captured by his father. From there he set forward again and at the end of a full day's march encamped in the valley called by the Jews "Valley of Thorns." It is close to a village named Gabath Saul, which means "Saul's Hill," and is a distance of about three and one half miles from Jerusalem.

From here with some six hundred handpicked horsemen he rode forward to reconnoiter the city's strength and to test the mettle of the Jews. Would they, on seeing him, be terrified into surrender before a single blow was struck? So long as he rode along the highroad leading directly to the wall, no one appeared outside the gate, but when he turned off, a band of Jews suddenly broke through the cavalry and cut Titus off with a mere handful of his men. Titus wore neither helmet nor armor for he had gone forward, as I said, not to fight but to observe. Yet despite the hail of arrows discharged at him, not one touched him. Titus saw that his safety now depended solely on himself. He turned his horse's head and charged into the midst of his attackers, struggling to cut his way through back to his main party. With great prowess, he finally succeeded in rejoining his troops and safely returned to his camp.

The next day Titus advanced his camp to Scopus, or Lookout Hill, as the place is called, because from here was obtained the first view of the city and the grand pile of the Temple gleaming in the distance. Another encampment was set up three-quarters of a mile in the rear and a third at the Mount of Olives, which faces the city on the east and is separated from it by a deep, intervening ravine.

Model of a centurion, commander of a hundred Roman soldiers.
ALINARI

And now the civil war in Jerusalem was checked for the first time by the appearance of the Romans in full force. The rival parties started a sorry alliance and began to ask each other what they were waiting for. What had possessed them to let themselves be hemmed in by these three fortified encampments? The Romans, without interference, were building fortified positions as strong as the city itself, while the Jews sat behind their battlements, like spectators, their hands and weapons idle! Shouting encouragements to each other, the rival factions joined forces. They dashed out suddenly against the Tenth Legion, racing across the ravine with bloodcurdling cries. They fell upon the Romans, who were working on their fortifications in scattered groups, their arms laid aside. The Romans, taken by surprise, were thrown into disorder and driven from their camp. In all probability the entire legion would have been destroyed if Titus had not instantly come to their aid.

70 A.D.

However, as soon as a temporary lull developed in the war outside the walls, there was a renewal of the factional strife within the city. When the Day of Unleavened Bread came round, the legendary anniversary of the Jews' first liberation from Egypt, Eleazar and his men opened the gates of the inner Temple just enough to allow in citizens who desired to worship. John made the festival a cloak for his own treacherous designs and armed many of his followers with concealed weapons and had them admitted into the Temple as worshippers. Once within they cast off their disguises and revealed themselves as men in arms. There was the utmost disorder and confusion around the Sanctuary, and many peaceable and innocent citizens were trampled under foot and brutally beaten with clubs and swords. John's followers, however, worked out a truce with the Zealots who had been in the inner chambers. John and Eleazar joined once again and together they now could defy Simon. The civil war thus was again reduced to two contending parties.

Meanwhile Titus decided to leave Scopus and encamp nearer the city. Behind a handpicked body of horse and foot soldiers strong enough to hold back sallies from the city, he ordered his main army to level all the intervening ground right up to the walls. Every fence and hedge was swept away, every fruit tree within the area felled. The hollows in the terrain were filled up, the jutting rocks smoothed with iron tools, and the whole space between Scopus and Herod's monuments, adjoining the spot called the Serpents' Pool, was flattened out to a dead level, a task which required four days. Titus himself pitched his camp a short distance from the walls of the city, just opposite the tower called Psephinus.

Jerusalem was fortified by three walls, except where it was enclosed by impassable ravines, where a single rampart was enough. The city was built on two hills facing each other and separated by a central valley. Of these hills, the one on which the Upper City was situated was far higher and with a straighter ridge than the other. Because of its strength it was called The Stronghold by King David, the father of Solomon who first built the Temple. We call it the Upper Agora or Market. The second hill, named Acra or The Citadel, was the site of the Lower City. On the outside, the two hills were protected by deep ravines and precipitous cliffs, which made access to the

Jerusalem at the time of the Second Temple

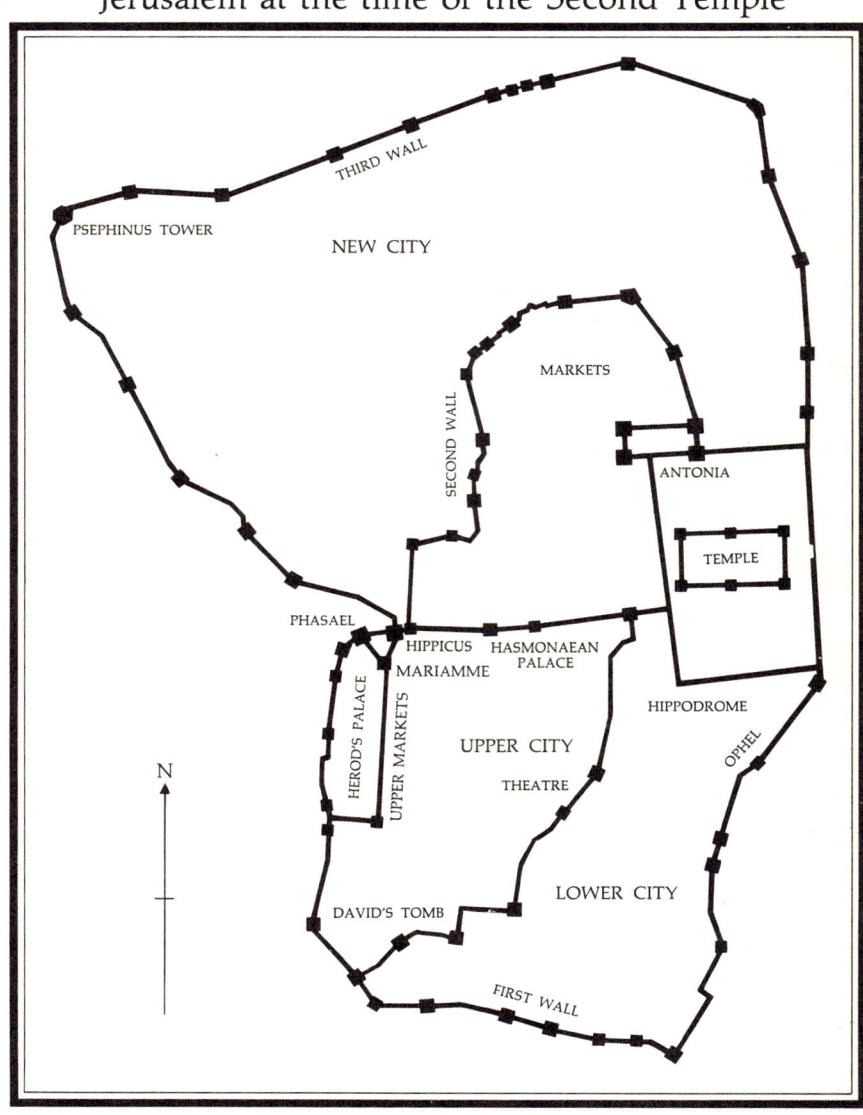

town impossible on every side. Of the three walls the most ancient was almost impregnable—David and Solomon and their successors on the throne had taken great pride in its construction. The second wall enclosed only the northern district of the town. The third was built by Agrippa I to enclose the newer sections of the city which had become quite defenseless, as the town, overflowing with inhabitants, had gradually crept beyond its protecting walls. Above the walls rose towers, thirty feet broad and thirty high, square and solid as the wall itself, with stones joined together perfectly, just as in the Temple itself. The third wall had ninety of these towers, separated at intervals of a hundred yards. The line of the middle wall was broken by fourteen towers, that of the old by sixty. The whole circumference of the city was 3¾ miles.

But wonderful as was the third wall, still more so was the tower Psephinus, opposite which Titus was encamped. It was 105 feet high and afforded a view embracing both Arabia and the farthermost boundaries of Jewish territory as far as the sea. It was eight-sided in form. Other towers built by Herod were: Hippicus, named after the king's friend, which was 120 feet high; a second tower, named Phasael after Herod's brother, which, with sumptuous apartments and bath, was 135 feet high. Here Simon made his headquarters. The third tower, Mariamme, named for Herod's queen, was far more luxurious and ornate than the others, as befitted a memorial to a woman.

Adjoining these towers, and protected by them, was the king's palace, a building which baffles all description. Indeed, its magnificence and furnishings were unsurpassed. It was completely enclosed by a wall forty-five feet high, broken at equal distances by ornamental towers. It contained immense banquet halls and bedrooms for one hundred guests. However, it is impossible to describe the palace adequately, and the memory of it is painful, recalling as it does the ravages of the fires set by the rebels in Jerusalem.

The Temple, originally situated on a strong hill surrounded by precipitous cliffs, contained very little level area, at first barely enough for the Sanctuary and the Altar. But in the course of ages, the hilltop was leveled and extended. Later the north wall was broken down, and thus all the area which subsequently became the whole Temple enclosure was doubled. Where its foundations were lowest, they built up from a depth of 450 feet, and, at some spots, even more. Blocks of stone measuring sixty feet were used. The superstructure itself was worthy of such foundations. The porticoes, all in double rows, were supported by columns 37½ feet high, each cut from a single block of the purest white marble. The ceilings were paneled with cedar. The natural magnificence of these columns, their excellent polish and perfect joining presented a striking spectacle, even without decorations of painting or sculpture.

No foreigner was permitted to enter the Holy Place, as the second enclosure of the Temple was called. Of the gates leading to the inner areas, nine were completely overlaid with gold and silver, as were their doorposts and lintels. One, outside the Sanctuary, was of Corinthian bronze and far more valuable than those plated with silver or even those set in gold. The sacred edifice itself, the Holy Temple, situated in the center, was approached by a flight of twelve steps. The first gate opening into the building was completely overlaid with gold, as was the whole wall around it. Above it were golden vines, from which hung grape clusters as big as a man. Before these doors hung a curtain of Babylonian tapestry, with embroidery of fine linen, blue, scarlet and purple, wrought with marvelous skill. The mystic meanings of the mixture of materials typified the universe. The scarlet seemed to represent fire, the linen the earth, blue the air, and purple the sea. Passing within, one found oneself on the ground floor of the Sanctuary, ninety feet high and the same in length. This length was divided too. The first portion was partitioned off at sixty feet and contained three of the most wonderful works of art known throughout the world: a lampstand, a table, and an altar of incense. The seven lamps, branching off the lampstand, represented the planets. The twelve loaves on the table were the symbols of the circle of the zodiac and the year; and the altar of incense, with its thirteen fragrant spices gathered from both sea and land, signified that all things are from God and for God. The innermost recess, measuring the remaining thirty feet, was screened from the outer portion by a curtain. In this stood nothing whatever. It was unapproachable, inviolable, invisible to all. It was called the Holy of Holies.

The strength of the combatants within Jerusalem at this time was as follows. Simon had an army, exclusive of the Idumaeans, of ten thousand men. Over these were fifty officers, Simon himself being the commander-in-chief. His Idumaean contingent numbered five thousand, under the command of ten officers. John, when he seized the Temple, had an army of six

A lute and a grape cluster, symbolizing the Temple. Coins of the Second Revolt (132–135 A.D.).

thousand men, commanded by twenty officers. Later the Zealots, having given up their fight with John, added to his numbers 2,400 men, led by Eleazar, their former chief.

But, now even with the Romans encamped beneath the walls, the civil strife did not slacken. The brief return to comparative unity and sanity, when the first Roman attack took place, was followed by a relapse, and the parties fell to fighting among themselves once more. Certainly they suffered nothing worse at the hands of the Romans than what they inflicted upon each other. For I maintain that it was the internal strife that overthrew the city, and I say that all the tragedy that befell the city may be blamed on her own people. The Romans had justice on their side. But let everyone follow his own opinion wherever the facts may lead him.

Outside the walls, Titus with some handpicked cavalry made a tour of inspection, looking for the best point for his attack. He decided to concentrate near the tomb of John Hyrcanus, the High Priest, for here the walls were on lower ground. The siege began with his order to the legions to lay waste to the outlying districts of the city in order to collect timber and to erect earthworks. The Jews did not permit the Romans to raise these earthworks unmolested. By every feat of ingenuity and daring, they strove night and day to stop them. Then the battering rams were brought up and Titus gave the order to strike. From three different quarters a frightful din echoed around the city. Seeing the common danger, both parties again joined in a common defense. As one body again, the Jews hurled showers of firebrands at the Roman machines, keeping the bat-

OPPOSITE:
Model of Roman assault platforms, towers, and protected passageways.
MUSEUM DELLA CIVILTA ROMANA

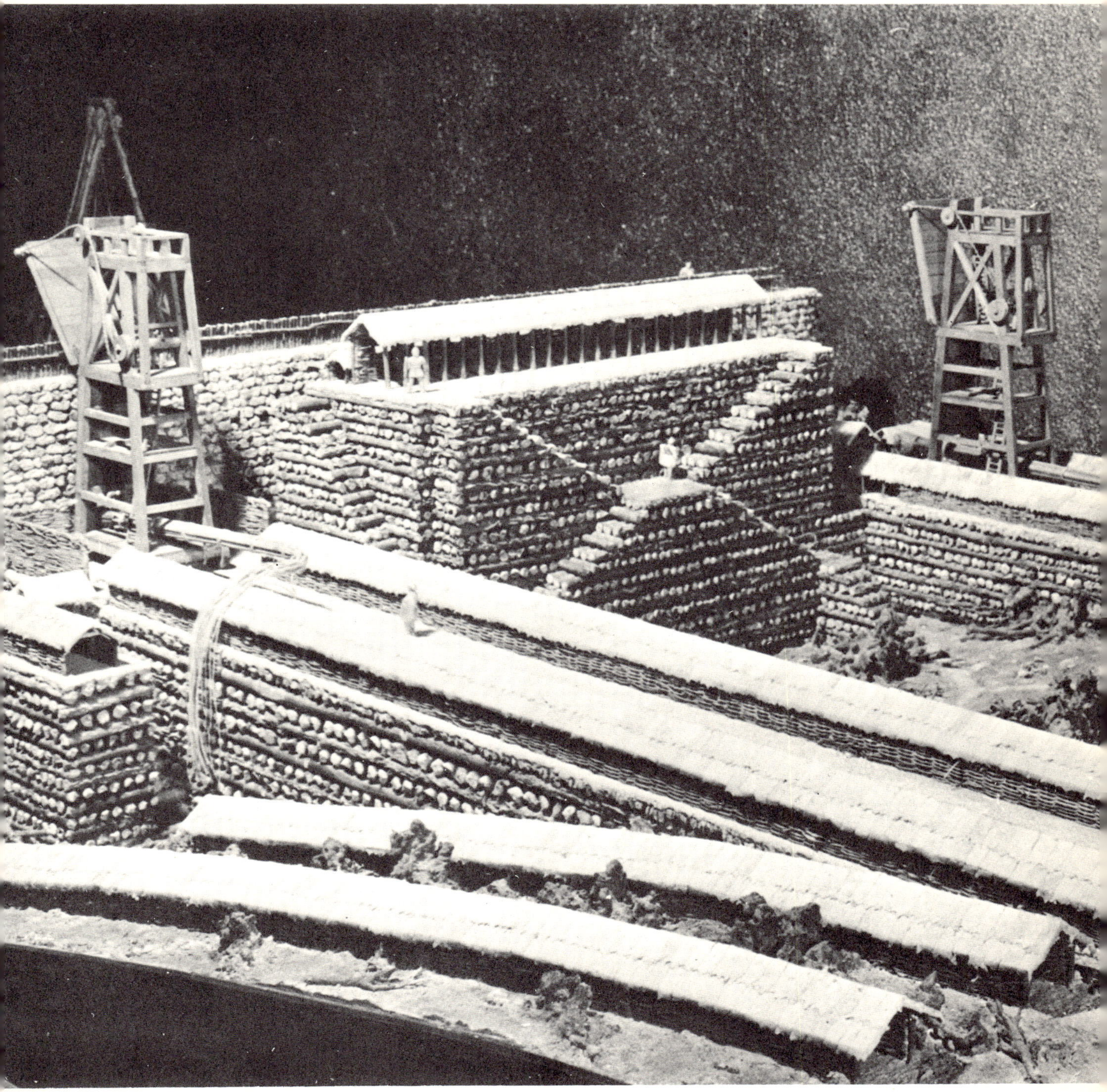

A model of a battering ram.
MUSEUM DELLA CIVILTA ROMANA. ALINARI

tering engines under constant fire. The more daring dashed out in bands and attacked the battering rams, falling on their crews and generally overpowering them. Titus, however, invariably rushed to the relief of those who were hard pressed and drove off the incendiaries, beat back the assailants on the walls, and got the battering rams back into action. But, in spite of all these efforts, the wall did not succumb to the blows.

The Jews watched for an opportunity to destroy the rams and suddenly dashed out, carrying firebrands to burn the Roman engines. In this engagement, Jewish courage at first was too quick for Roman discipline. A furious conflict started around the Roman war engines, one side striving its utmost to set them afire, the other straining to prevent it. The fire was gaining hold and the whole Roman fortification would probably have perished in flames, had not the picked troops from Alexandria finally stood firm, holding off the Jewish attackers until Titus and the flower of his cavalry charged and pushed them back.

Titus ordered three towers constructed, each seventy-five feet high, from which he could bombard the defenders on the walls of the city. The Jews suffered severely as the result of these towers, for from them the defenders became targets for Roman lighter artillery, javelin-men, archers, and stone-throwers. These towers were so tall that they were out of range of Jewish weapons. They were so solid that they could not easily be overturned, and they were encased in iron so that they could not be set on fire. On the other hand, if the Jews withdrew out of range of the missiles from the towers, they could no longer check the impact of the battering rams, whose incessant pounding was gradually taking effect. At last the wall began to crumble before "Victor," as the Jews themselves called the largest of the Roman engines because of its long history of successes. Moreover, because of laziness or just their usual bad judgment, the Jews decided not to defend the third wall, since there were still two other walls behind it. Thus on the fifteenth day of the siege, the Romans became masters of the outer wall, mounting through the breach which Victor had made. Titus razed a large part of the wall as well as the northern quarter of the city.

Titus now shifted his camp within the first wall and proceeded immediately to attack the second bastion. The Jews main-

c. *May 25, 70 A.D.*

tained a stubborn defense. But five days after the capture of the first wall, Titus stormed the second. He made his entry with a thousand legionaries and his own picked troops through a narrow breach in the wall in that district of the new town where the wool shops, the smithies, and the cloth markets were located. The district was all narrow alleys, leading from the walls at many different angles. The Jewish defenders counterattacked inside the wall. Knowing the narrow streets, they surprised the Romans, wounded multitudes of them, and drove them back to the breach in the wall. The entire invading force would probably have been cut to pieces had not Titus come to its rescue. Posting archers at the ends of the streets, he kept the Jews at bay with showers of arrows until his soldiers had all retired safely back through the wall.

The Jews were carried away by their success in repelling the Romans from the city. But they were blind to the strength of the Romans. They could not see, either, the signs of famine beginning to show themselves in the city. For three days they maintained their stubborn defense and held their ground, but on the fourth, unable to hold back a massive assault by Titus, they were compelled to fall back again. Titus, once more in possession of the wall, immediately razed the whole northern portion of it. He began at once to plan for an attack on the third wall.

Titus now decided to suspend the siege operations for a while to see if the demolition of the second wall and the threat of famine might not lead to a truce and a surrender. He used the delay to his own advantage as follows. Pay day for the soldiers arrived, so Titus ordered his officers to parade the forces

OPPOSITE:
A Roman emperor addressing his troops.
ARCH OF CONSTANTINE, ROME. ANDERSON

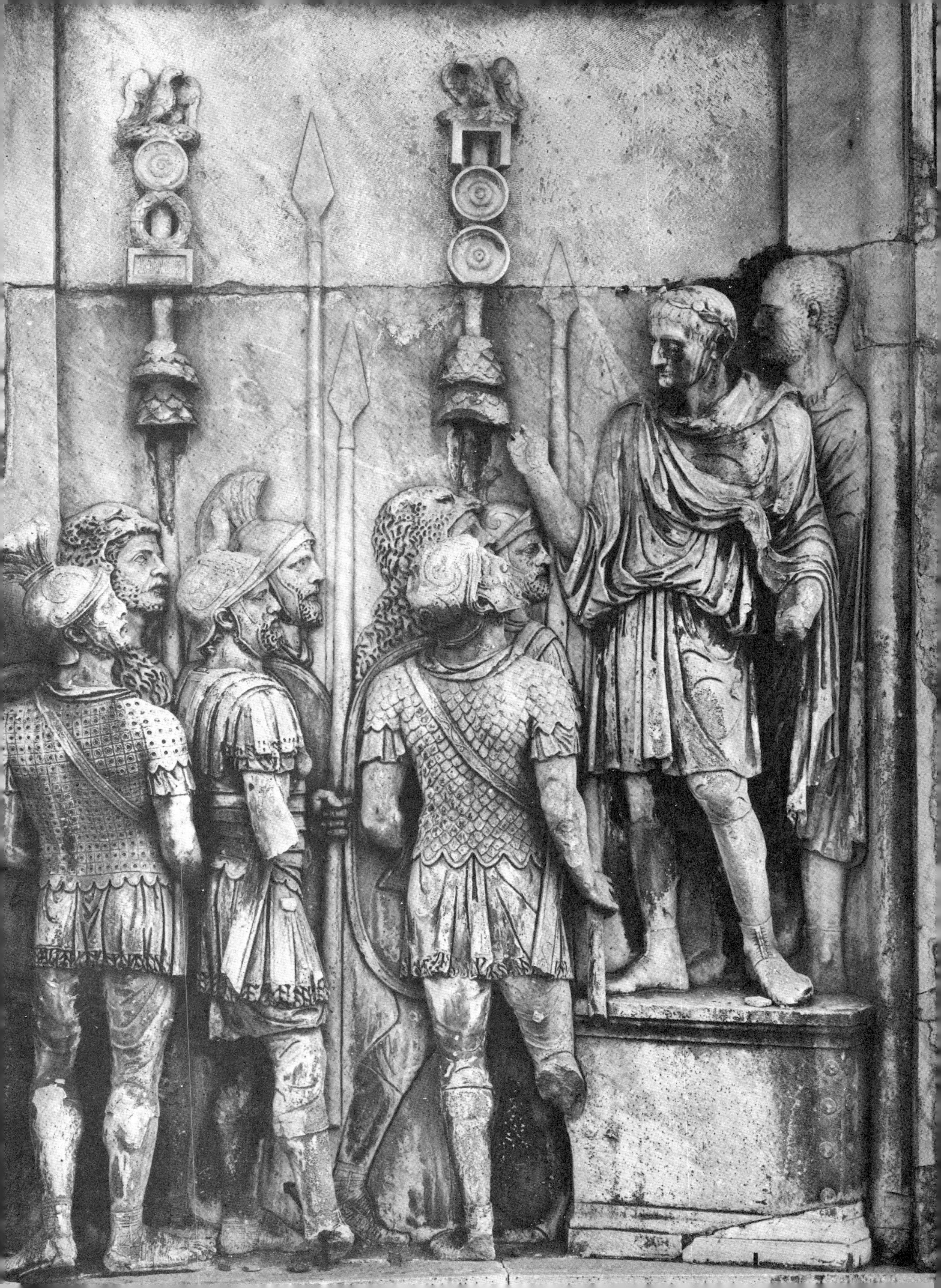

in full view of the besieged and there count out the money to each man. The troops, as usual, drew forth their arms and advanced richly clad in mail. The cavalrymen led their horses, all decked out and richly caparisoned. The whole area in front of the city gleamed with silver and gold. All of the old wall and the north side of the Temple were thronged with spectators. The houses behind the wall could be seen packed with craning heads. There was not a single spot that was not jammed with people. Even the boldest were struck with dismay at the sight of this muster of the Roman forces, the might of their arms, and the splendid discipline of the men. It took four days for the several Roman legions to receive their pay. On the fifth, since no overtures for peace had come from the Jews, Titus began building earthworks for the assault on the Upper Town and the Temple. In the meanwhile, he neglected no opportunity to urge the Jews to reconsider their rebellion against Rome. He even delegated me, Josephus, to parley with the defenders in our native tongue, thinking that they might yield more readily to the persuasions of a fellow-countryman.

Accordingly, I, Josephus, went round the walls, keeping well out of range of the Jewish artillerymen but still within hearing distance. I repeatedly implored them to spare themselves and the people, their country and their Temple. During my appeals I was derided by many from the ramparts and reviled by others. Failing to move my people by direct advice, I turned to a review of the history of the Jews and the lessons to be learned from it. I showed them how God had passed over to the side of the Romans, and I offered to surrender my own life and that of my

The Romans, defending a fortified city.
COLUMN OF TRAJAN, ROME.
GERMAN ARCHAEOLOGICAL INSTITUTE

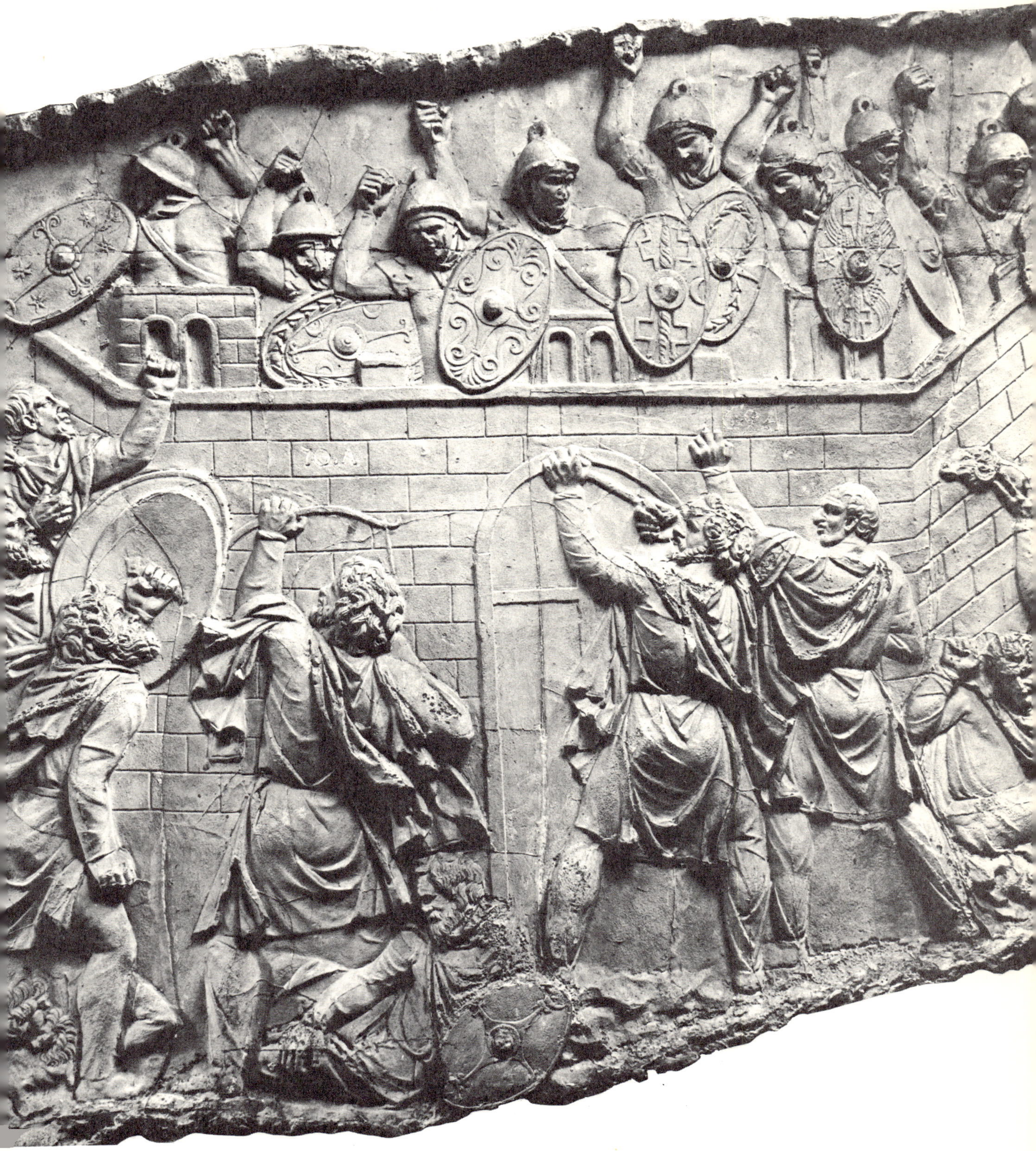

mother, wife, and family if it would make them spare the city and nation. But, despite my tears and my strong appeals, the insurgents would not budge from their doomed course.

Some people, however, were incited to desert. They sold all their belongings and their most valuable treasures for whatever they could get and then swallowed the gold coins to prevent robbery. Inside the city, the frenzy of the defenders increased as the famine grew more terrible. Hunger destroys all human feelings, and most of all, any sense of decency. Wives would snatch food from husbands, children from fathers, and—most pitiable sight of all—mothers from the very mouths of their babes.

c. June 16, 70 A.D.

Meanwhile, the earthworks of Titus were progressing, notwithstanding the galling fire from the ramparts to which the Romans were exposed. The earthworks were completed only after seventeen days of continuous toil. While the engines of war were being brought into position, John of Gischala, from within the city, undermined the ground right up to the Roman earthworks. He dug tunnels underground, supporting them with wooden props. Then he set fire to these supports so that the entire tunnel collapsed. With a thunderous crash the Roman earthworks fell in. The Romans were in despair over this sudden catastrophe and discouraged by the ingenuity of the Jewish defenders. Two days later at another point, Simon's party launched an attack on the other Roman earthworks, for the besiegers had brought up the battering rams and were already pounding at the wall. The Jews attacked with fervor and nothing could stop them until they set fire to the war machines. The flames shot high and the Romans came rushing from their encampments to the rescue. The fire spread, enveloping the Romans in flames. They beat a retreat to their camp, with the Jews in hot pursuit after them. Only the appearance of Titus with his elite force, attacking the Jews in the flank, turned the tide of battle, sending the Jewish host back in retreat to the city. The Romans, however, their earthworks demolished, were downhearted. In one hour they had lost the fruit of long labor.

Titus now held a council of war with his officers. The more warlike advised storming the wall with every ounce of force. The more cautious urged the reconstruction of the earthworks or the establishment of a total blockade of the city. Titus did not want to remain inactive, fearing that some of the splendor of victory would be lost in too long a delay. So, moving with both speed and safety, he ordered a wall thrown around the whole city, blocking every exit. Thus the Jews would be forced to surrender in despair or be wasted by famine. The Jews were now unable to leave the city. All hope of escape was now cut off. The famine, growing greater and greater, devoured whole families. The roofs were thronged with completely exhausted women and infants; the alleys with corpses of the aged. Children and youths, their stomachs swollen from hunger, roamed like phantoms through the market places and collapsed wherever their doom overtook them. But the rebels were unmoved by the sufferings of the people.

Titus, anxious to save some of the famine-stricken people, decided to quicken his activities. He ordered an earthwork position erected opposite the fortress of Antonia. The timber for it

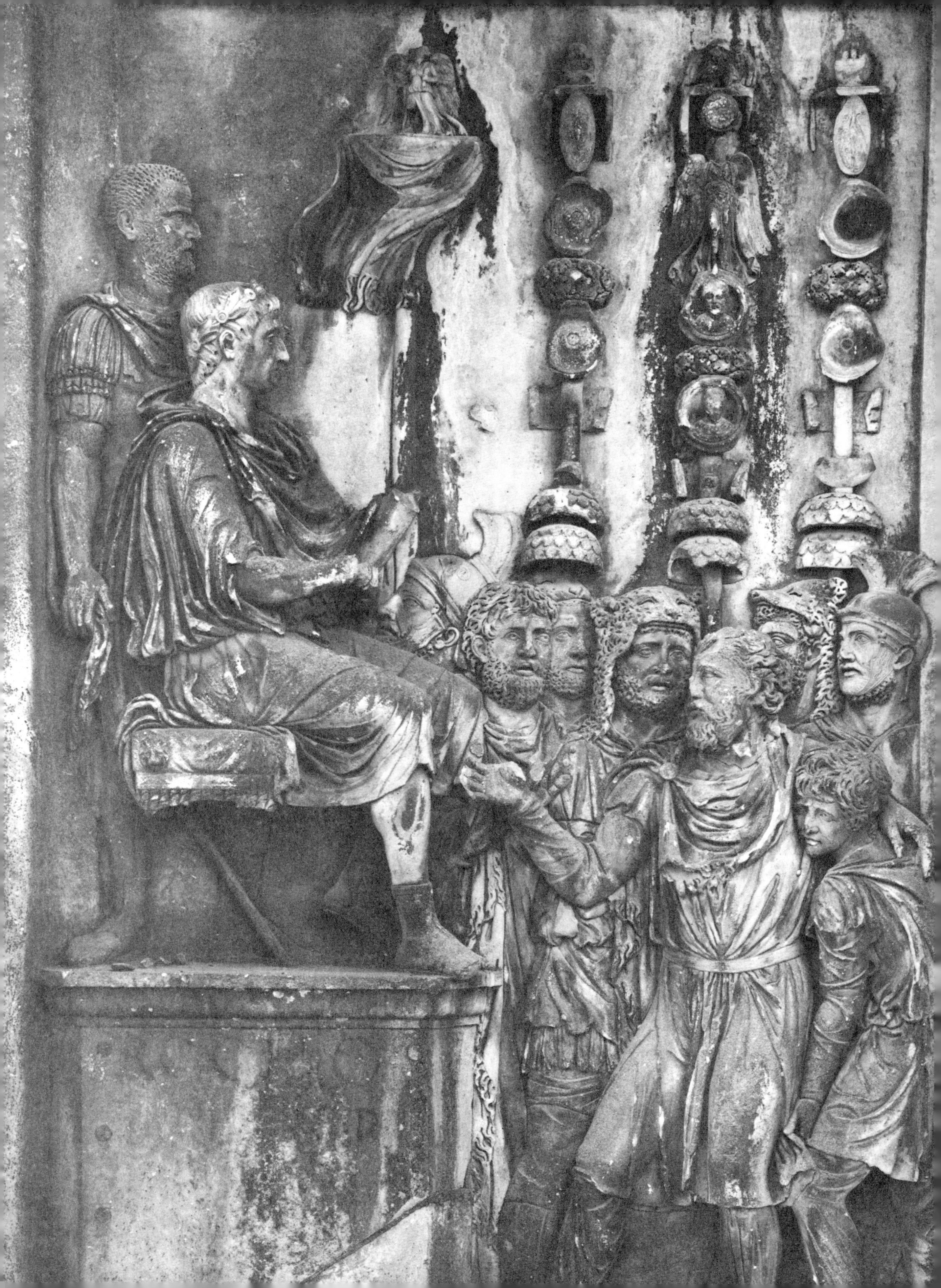

was assembled with much difficulty since all the trees around the city had already been felled for the previous works. The new material came from a distance of ten miles.

Inside Jerusalem, Simon turned on the very men who had invited him into the city, charging them with conspiring with the Romans and condemning them to instant execution. John, when he could no longer squeeze further booty from the people, turned to the Temple and melted down many of the offering plates, the bowls, salvers, and tables, even the ones sent by Augustus Caesar and his wife many years before. John told his fellows, as they appropriated these precious offerings, that they should not shrink from using divine things to defend the Divinity. Those who fought for the Temple deserve to be supported by it, he said.

Meanwhile death stalked the city, taking its toll from rich and poor. Refugees who managed to get to Titus reported that the corpses of the lower classes, which were thrown out of the city through the gates, amounted to 600,000, while of the other classes the number of dead was impossible to determine. They told Titus that, with the city all walled in, some of the people were reduced to such straits that they searched the sewers and ate what once would have disgusted them just to look at. The tale of these horrors aroused the pity of the Romans. Yet the rebels, who saw them with their own eyes, would not relent. They were blinded by Fate, which, both for Jerusalem and for themselves, was now at hand.

The Romans, meanwhile, despite great difficulty in collecting timber, completed their earthwork platforms in twenty-one

OPPOSITE:
A defeated enemy chieftain submits to a Roman emperor.
ARCH OF CONSTANTINE, ROME. ANDERSON

days. They had cleared the whole district around Jerusalem for a distance of ten miles, making the sight of the countryside pitiful to behold, reduced as it was from a lovely vista of parks and woods to utter desert, stripped bare of trees. No one, who had ever seen the once beautiful suburbs of the Judean capital, could have held back tears or suppressed a sigh at the sight of her present desolation.

John of Gischala and the Zealots in the fortress of Antonia mounted an attack on the new earthworks, hoping to prevent the battering rams from being brought up. They advanced with torches but turned back, with little evidence of their formerly bold fighting spirit. There seemed to be no plan of attack. They dashed out in small parties, irregularly, hesitating, alarmed—in short, not like Jews. The characteristics of the nation—daring, impetuosity, the concerted charge, the refusal to retreat even when defeated—all were lacking. The Romans thereupon brought up the siege engines and set them up, braving the rain of rocks, iron, and every species of missile poured down upon them by the Jews. The Romans redoubled their efforts, but the walls resisted the battering blows. The Romans then sent another party, with crowbars, to undermine the defending walls. It succeeded only in dislodging four stones.

During the night, that part of the wall where the rams were pounding, weakened further by the cave-in of the tunnels dug under it previously by John, suddenly collapsed and fell to the ground. To everyone's surprise the Romans were not overjoyed by this good fortune, but instead were downcast by the discovery of a second wall which had been built behind it.

Four days later, by a secret night attack on the sentinels guarding the tower of Antonia, the Romans reached their goal. Titus and his body of picked men quickly mounted to the top of the wall. The Jews abandoned the tower and fled into the Temple, into which the Romans were also penetrating by using the very tunnels which John had previously dug.

The followers of John and Simon, son of Gioras, drawn up on two sides, sought to block the Roman advance with mighty feats of strength and courage. So the armies clashed in a life and death struggle around the entrances of the Temple. The quarters were so close that missiles and spears were useless to both sides. Drawing their swords, they closed with each other

The Romans attacking on foot and on horseback.
COLUMN OF TRAJAN, ROME.
GERMAN ARCHAEOLOGICAL INSTITUTE

July 24, 70 A.D.

August, 70 A.D.

and in the jumbled melee it was impossible to tell friend from foe. At length Jewish fury prevailed over Roman skill and the whole line began to waver. The Romans fell back, considering it sufficient for the moment to have won the fortress of Antonia. Titus now ordered his troops to raze this fortification and to use its stones to build a roadway for the ascent of the whole army to the Temple.

On that day it was learned that the perpetual ceremonies of sacrifice in the Temple had been discontinued. I, Josephus, was instructed by Titus to urge the Jews to preserve the ceremonials of the Holy Place and to resume the interrupted sacrifices. Standing so that my words would reach not only John, the leader of the Zealots, but the multitude as well, I delivered Titus' message in our native language with earnest appeals to them to save our country from destruction and to stamp out the flames which were already licking at the gates of the Sanctuary. But John spurned my plea, claiming he "could never fear capture, since the city was God's." At this I cried aloud, "Pure indeed have you kept it for God! Even so, it is no disgrace to change your ways, even at the final moment!" And I recited the example of a Jewish king of old who voluntarily abandoned the city to keep it from falling into enemy hands. I even promised John a pardon from the Romans, but he and his followers paid no heed. Titus, himself, came out and upbraided John and his men, offering to spare the Temple. But the offer was treated with contempt as a sign of cowardice, not goodwill, on the part of Titus.

Titus, thereupon, resumed hostilities. He could not bring

up his whole strength because of the limited space, so he chose a select force and ordered an attack by night. He stood on the battlements and watched the struggle. Under their commander's eye, the Romans vied man with man and company with company, each competing for honors and promotions. The contest was confined by the choked space, like a battle on a stage in a theater. At length, the struggle broke off, neither side having seriously repelled the other. Victory remained in the balance.

The rest of the Roman army spent seven days dismantling the stonework of the fortress, Antonia, to prepare a roadway up to the Temple. When the legions had completed this roadway, Titus ordered the rams brought up opposite the western hall of the outer court of the Temple. Before these rams were set in position, the mightiest of the Roman siege engines had for six days battered the wall without effect. Another band of Romans tried to undermine the foundations of the Northern Gate, but it stood firm. Finally, despairing all attempts with engines and crowbars, the Romans brought up ladders to scale the walls and porticoes. The Romans tried to mount these ladders. Some climbed up with the battle standards and defended them fiercely, since their capture by the Jews would be a disaster and a disgrace. Nevertheless the Jews wrested these standards from their hands and captured them. Every Roman who had tried to scale the walls was destroyed.

Titus, who had been trying to spare the Holy Temple from direct assault, now saw that his efforts had led only to the injury of his own troops. He therefore issued orders to set the gates of the Temple on fire. This was done and all that day the

c. August 27, 70 A.D.

c. *August 28, 70 A.D.* fires raged. On the following day, Titus ordered the fires put out to make way for the advance of the legions. At the same time he assembled his generals and brought up for discussion the subject of the Temple. Some of Titus' lieutenants demanded that the Temple be treated with all the severity of the rules of warfare. They contended that the Temple should be destroyed since it would remain a rallying point for the Jews as long as it stood. Others were more lenient, suggesting that the Temple should be spared if it was not used as a fortress, otherwise it should be burned. Titus, however, declared that even if the Jews were to use the Temple for military purposes, he would not wreak vengeance on a building. Besides under no circumstance did he desire to burn down so magnificent an edifice, since it would be an ornament to the Empire if it stood.

c. *August 29, 70 A.D.* Throughout that day, fatigue and fear crushed the Jews. But on the following day, with strength and courage renewed, they returned to the attack, making the Roman line bend under their fury. Titus brought up his special cavalry, whose onset the Jews could not withstand. Yet, whenever the Romans retired, the Jews returned to the attack, only to fall back once again when the Romans wheeled around. Titus then determined to throw in his entire strength on the following day and invest the Temple. That building, it seems, had been condemned to the flames long ago; for here, after the passing of many years,

c. *August 30, 70 A.D.* there came that fateful day, the tenth of the month of Ab, the same day on which of old it had been burned by King Nebuchadnezzar of Babylon.

When Titus left the battlefield, the Jewish rebels again

attacked and a fierce engagement ensued between the Temple defenders and the Roman troops, who had been ordered to put out the flames in the Temple gates. The Romans were pursuing their opponents right up to the Sanctuary itself, when one of the Roman soldiers, acting without orders, snatched a burning brand and, climbing on the back of one of his fellows, tossed the fiery missile through a low golden door, which led to the chambers surrounding the Holy Place. As the flames shot up, a cry, as heartrending as the tragedy, arose from the Jews, who rushed to save the sacred building.

Titus was resting in his tent when a messenger rushed in with the news that the Temple was burning. Starting up just as he was, he rushed to the Temple to stop the conflagration. Behind him came his whole staff of generals, followed by a large contingent of excited legionaries, all confused and shouting. Titus, by voice and gesture, signalled to his soldiers to put out the fires, but they neither heard his shouts nor heeded his commands. The legionaries who had come up with Titus plunged into the fray, pretending not even to hear his orders and encouraging the forward parties to throw in even more firebrands. There was a huge crush around the doorways and many were trampled down by their own companions. Many stumbled on the hot smoldering ruins, suffering the same fate as the defenders. Around the altar, a pile of corpses grew higher and higher. Down the steps of the Sanctuary flowed a stream of blood. Titus, unable to restrain the frenzy of his troops and to prevent the fire from gaining the upper hand, rushed into the Temple itself with his generals and examined the Holy Place and all that it contained. The flames had not yet reached the interior, so Titus assumed that the structure still might be saved. He hastened outside and personally appealed to his troops to quench the fires. But the men, swept away by their fury, their hatred of the Jews, and their hope for rich plunder, refused to pay heed to him.

The tragic end was precipitated by one trooper who had entered the building and, when Titus dashed out to hold back his soldiers, thrust a firebrand into the inner gate. At once a flame shot up from the interior. Titus and his generals departed. Thus against the Roman leader's wishes, the Temple was set on fire.

Deeply as we must mourn for that most marvelous edifice, yet may we draw great comfort from the thought that the Temple was as bound by fate as a living being. One may well marvel at the exactness of Destiny's cycle, which waited until the very month and the very day on which in bygone times the Temple had been burned by the Babylonians. From its first foundation by King Solomon up to its destruction, which took place in the second year of Vespasian's reign, the total period amounted to 1,130 years, 7 months, and 15 days. And from its rebuilding in the second year of the reign of Cyrus of Persia until its fall under Vespasian, the time was 639 years and 45 days.

While the Temple blazed, the victors plundered everything that came their way and slaughtered wholesale all whom they caught. No pity was shown for age, no reverence for rank. Children and graybeards, laity and priests, all were massacred. The roar of the flames mingled with the groans of the falling

The columned facade of the Sanctuary of the Temple on a coin minted during the Second Jewish Revolt (132–135 A.D.).
FOTOTECA UNIONE

victims. The din was deafening. The war cries of the Roman legions, sweeping onward in a mass, mixed with the howls of the rebels, encircled by fire and sword, and the shrieks of the people, fleeing panic-stricken into the arms of their enemies.

The Romans, thinking it useless to spare the surrounding buildings now that the Temple was afire, set them all alight. They burned the treasury chambers and the one remaining portico of the outer court, on which six thousand people, mostly women and children, had taken refuge. Some were killed plunging out of the flames; others perished amidst them. Out of all that multitude not a soul escaped.

The defending rebels managed to make their way through the Roman lines and with great difficulty forced their way out of the Temple and from there to the city. Now that the rebels were gone, the Romans marched their standards into the Temple

The Western Wall of the Second Temple, known also as the Wailing Wall, which is still standing in Jerusalem.
FOTOTECA UNIONE

court and set them up opposite the Eastern Gate. There they made sacrifices and, with rousing cheers and thunderous acclamations, hailed Titus as the victor.

Simon and John, now vanquished on all sides in battle and shut in by the wall which prevented their escape, invited Titus to a parley. Titus appeared with his troops, whose anger and weapons he ordered kept in check. Since he was the conqueror, he exercised the victor's right and spoke first.

"Are you content now, gentlemen, with the sufferings of your country? With utter disregard for our strength and your weakness, you have brought destruction upon your people, your city and your Temple. You deserve the destruction that now hangs over you.

"However if you throw down your arms and give yourselves up, I will grant you your lives."

To this Simon and John replied that they had pledged themselves never to surrender. Instead they asked permission to pass through his lines with their wives and children, undertaking to retire to the desert and leave the city to him. Titus was outraged that men, no better than prisoners, should make demands to him as though they were victors. He ordered it proclaimed that they could no longer hope for any terms, but that they should fight with all their might and save themselves as best they could, because he would now exact what was his due as the conqueror.

Titus gave his troops permission to burn and sack Jerusalem. The rebel forces rushed to the Royal Palace for safety. They were pursued by the Romans, who set the Lower City on fire.

September, 70 A.D.

I, Josephus, even at the last, never stopped begging the rebels to spare whatever was left of the city, but the response was always scorn and ridicule. The last hope for Simon and John and their remaining followers lay in the underground passages below the city, where they hoped they could find hiding places until the Romans departed.

The Upper City could not be subdued without erecting earthworks. After eighteen days of labor, these works were completed and again the Romans brought up their engines. A portion of the wall finally broke down, and some of the towers crumbled under the battering of the rams. The last few defenders took flight and found refuge in the sewers. At long last the Romans were masters of the walls. They planted their victorious standards on the towers. They had found the end of the

c. September 25, 70 A.D.

war much less bloody than the beginning. They could hardly believe it when they surmounted this last wall without losing a man.

Then the Romans poured into the streets and alleys of the Upper City, swords in hands, and massacred indiscriminately all they met, burning down the houses with all who had taken refuge within. When night fell, the fires had gotten the upper hand, and so perished Jerusalem in flames. Titus now issued orders to kill only those who were found under arms and offering resistance. All others he ordered taken prisoner. All the seditious and brigands, who informed on one another, were put to death. The tallest and handsomest of the youths were reserved for the triumphal procession in Rome. Of the rest, all over seventeen were sent in chains into slavery in Egypt, while many others were given by Titus to various provinces for gladiatorial combats with men and beasts. Those under seventeen were sold. The total number of prisoners taken throughout the war amounted to 97,000. And those who perished during the entire siege from the war, pestilence, and famine numbered 1,100,000.

Now the Romans instituted a search for those in the underground sewers. John, driven by hunger, finally begged for help for himself and his followers. The Romans sentenced him to life imprisonment. Simon, son of Gioras, had climbed into one of the secret underground passages with his most faithful friends and some experienced tunnelers, who brought along the tools of their craft. They followed the old tunnels and when they reached the end, they began digging, hoping to be able to keep on going. But soon they were exhausted. Simon tried to

An onyx cameo with the imperial eagle, Rome's symbol of power.
KUNSTHISTORISCHES MUSEUM, VIENNA

escape by a ruse, but he was captured by the Romans and thrown into chains. Titus, when he learned of Simon's capture, ordered the prisoner to be kept for the triumph, which would celebrate his victory in Rome.

Thus was Jerusalem taken in the second year of the reign of Vespasian. The city had been captured on five previous occasions. It was now for the second time utterly devastated. Asochaeus, King of Egypt, and after him, Antiochus and then Pompey, and subsequently Sossius in league with Herod, had taken the city but had spared it. Before their time, the king of Babylon had stormed it and laid it waste.

The original founder of the city was a Canaanite chief, called Melchi-Zedek, or king of righteousness in the holy tongue, for he was indeed such a ruler. The Canaanite population was expelled by David, king of the Jews, who established his own people there. Four hundred and seventy years and six months after his time, it was razed to the ground by the Babylonians. The period from King David, the first Jewish sovereign of Jerusalem, to its destruction by Titus was 1,179 years. From the city's first foundation until its final overthrow, the time elapsed was 2,177 years. Nevertheless, nothing could avert its ruin, not its great age, its wealth, its people spread all over the inhabited world, not even the glory of its religious heritage. Thus ended the siege of Jerusalem.

Titus ordered the whole city and the Temple, too, to be razed to the ground, leaving only the loftiest towers and a portion of the wall on the west as an encampment for the garrison which was to remain behind. All the rest was so completely

c. September 26, 70 A.D.

The Romans celebrated victories by staging spectacular games, often featuring daring chariot races.
FOLIGNO MUSEUM.
GERMAN ARCHAEOLOGICAL INSTITUTE

leveled to the ground as to leave future visitors no reason for believing that the place had ever been inhabited.

Titus then commended his troops for their valor and gave out awards and honors to all who had performed brilliant feats during the war. He placed crowns of gold upon their heads, presented them with golden neck chains, little golden spears, and standards made of silver. Each was promoted to a higher rank. When all had been rewarded, he invoked blessings upon the army and offered sacrifices of thanksgiving for his victory. Then with two legions, he returned to Caesarea, where he deposited the bulk of his spoils and directed that his prisoners be kept in custody. It was the winter season, so he could not sail to Italy. Titus traveled to Caesarea-Philippi where he remained for a considerable time, putting on all kinds of spectacular shows of Jewish prisoners being thrown to wild beasts or forced to fight one another to the death. He put on similar spectacles in all cities of Syria. He then set out for Egypt and, on the way, visited Jerusalem, contrasting the sorry scene of desolation with the former splendor of the city. From Alexandria he sent back his armies to their respective stations. He ordered Simon, son of Gioras, and John of Gischala and seven hundred other prisoners, selected as remarkable for their stature and beauty, to be transported to Italy, where he intended to exhibit them in the triumphal procession.

After a voyage as favorable as he could have desired, Rome gave him a reception and a welcome as it had given his father. Vespasian and his sons decided to celebrate their achievements by one triumphal procession in common. Vespasian's other son, Domitian, had settled disordered affairs in Gaul.

At the break of dawn, on the morning of the triumph in Rome, Vespasian and Titus, crowned with laurel and clad in traditional purple, walked forth to meet the senate and chief magistrates and those Romans of equestrian rank. A tribunal had been erected in front of the porticoes, with chairs of ivory on which Vespasian and his sons took their seats. Instantly cheers rose from the troops. Vespasian acknowledged the acclamations and signaled for silence. Amidst profound and universal stillness, he rose and, covering most of his head with his mantle, recited the customary prayers. Titus also prayed in like manner. Vespasian dismissed the soldiers to the customary breakfast provided for them by the emperors.

Vespasian then withdrew to the triumphal gate, which is so named because of the processions which always pass through it. Here the princes first broke their fast. They donned the triumphal robes, made sacrifices to the gods, whose statues stood

OVERLEAF:
The Arch of Titus in Rome commemorates the Roman victory over Judea. A panel depicts the triumphal procession.
ARCH OF TITUS, ROME. ALINARI

131

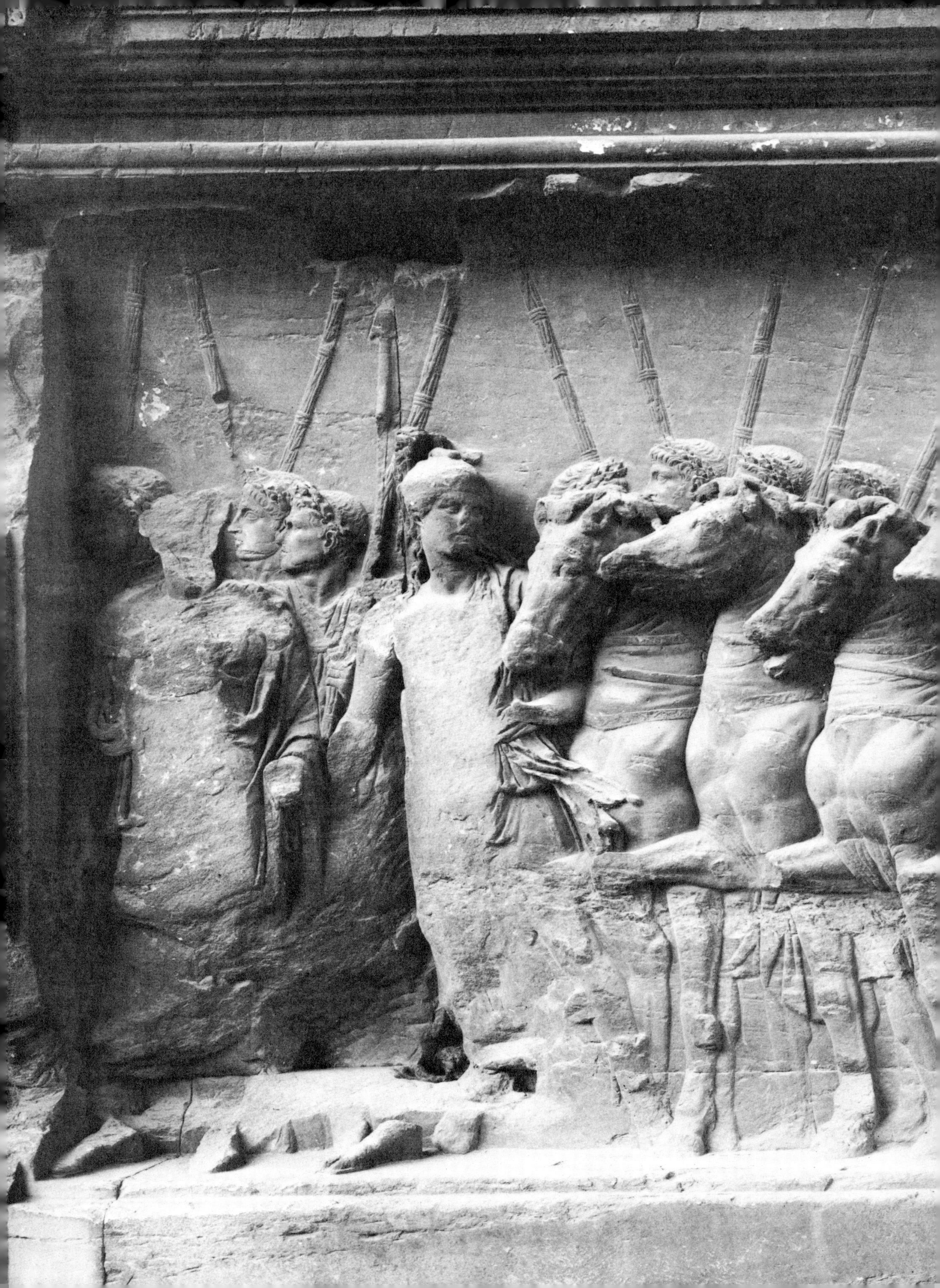

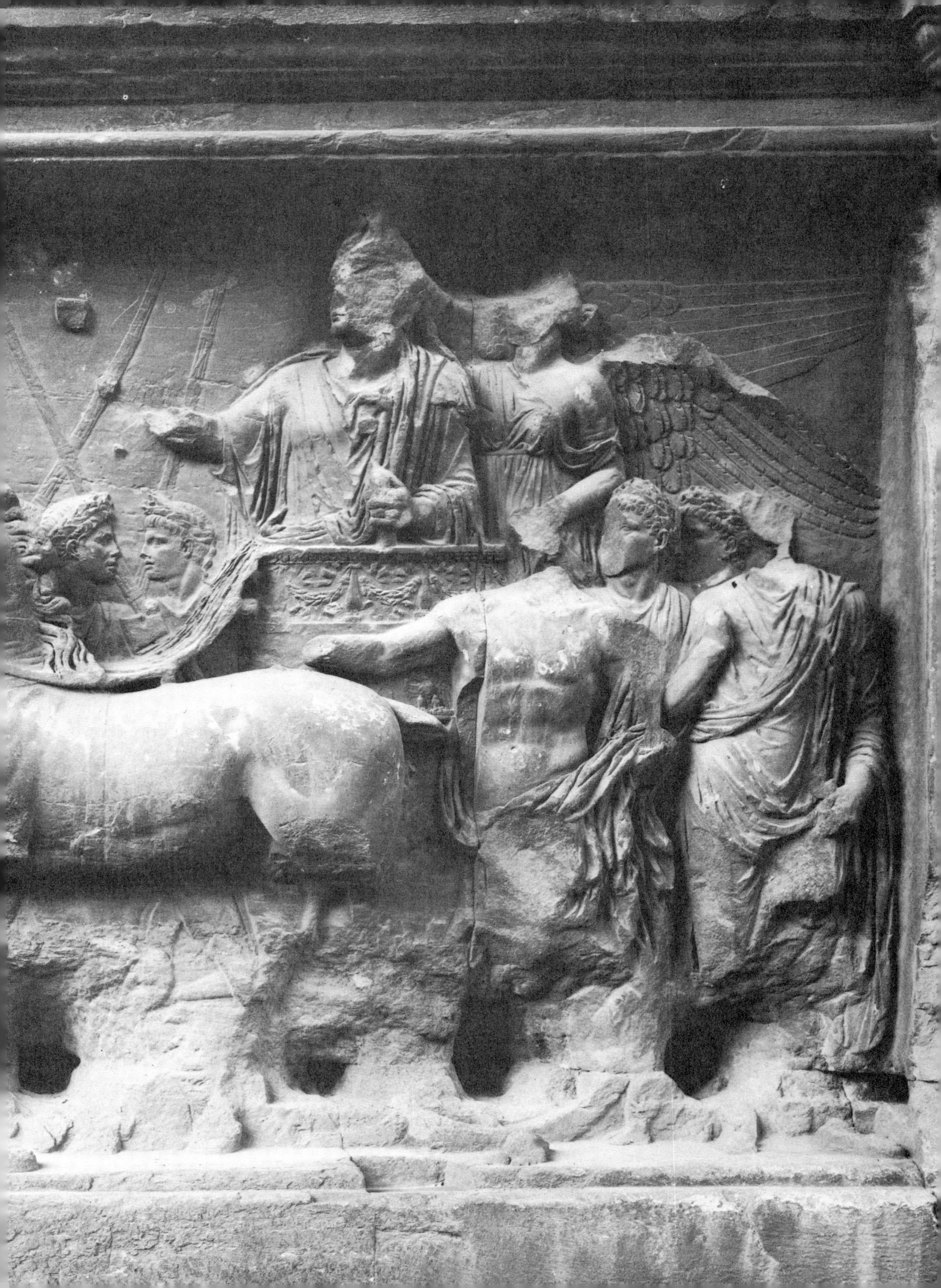

beside the gate, and sent the triumphal pageant on its way. The Emperor and his son drove off through the theatres in order to give the crowds a better view. It is impossible adequately to describe the magnificence of these spectacles. Silver and gold and ivory in huge masses, wrought in all manner of shapes, flowed along like a river. Tapestries, embroidered by Babylonian art, with perfect portraitures, were carried along. There were jewels, rare gems, statues of the Roman gods, beasts of many species, even the mob of captives dressed with variety and beauty to hide any bodily injury or disfigurement. But most astonishing were the moving stages, some three or four stories high, on which the war was depicted by numerous tableaux, in separate sections, providing a vivid picture of its episodes. On each stage was placed the commander of one of the conquered cities shown in the very attitude in which he was captured. A number of ships also followed.

But conspicuous above all the spoils stood out those captured in the Temple at Jerusalem. These consisted of a golden table, many talents in weight, and a lampstand, likewise made of gold. Affixed to the base of the lampstand was a central shaft, from which there extended seven slender branches, arranged like the prongs of a trident, each ending in a wrought lamp. After these, and last of all the spoils, was carried a copy of the Jewish Law. Then followed a large party carrying images of victory, all of ivory and gold. Behind them drove Vespasian, followed by Titus, while Domitian rode besides them, magnificently dressed, mounted on a horse that was itself a splendid sight.

OPPOSITE:
Jewish war captives carrying the booty from the Temple in the triumphal procession.
ARCH OF TITUS, ROME. ALINARI

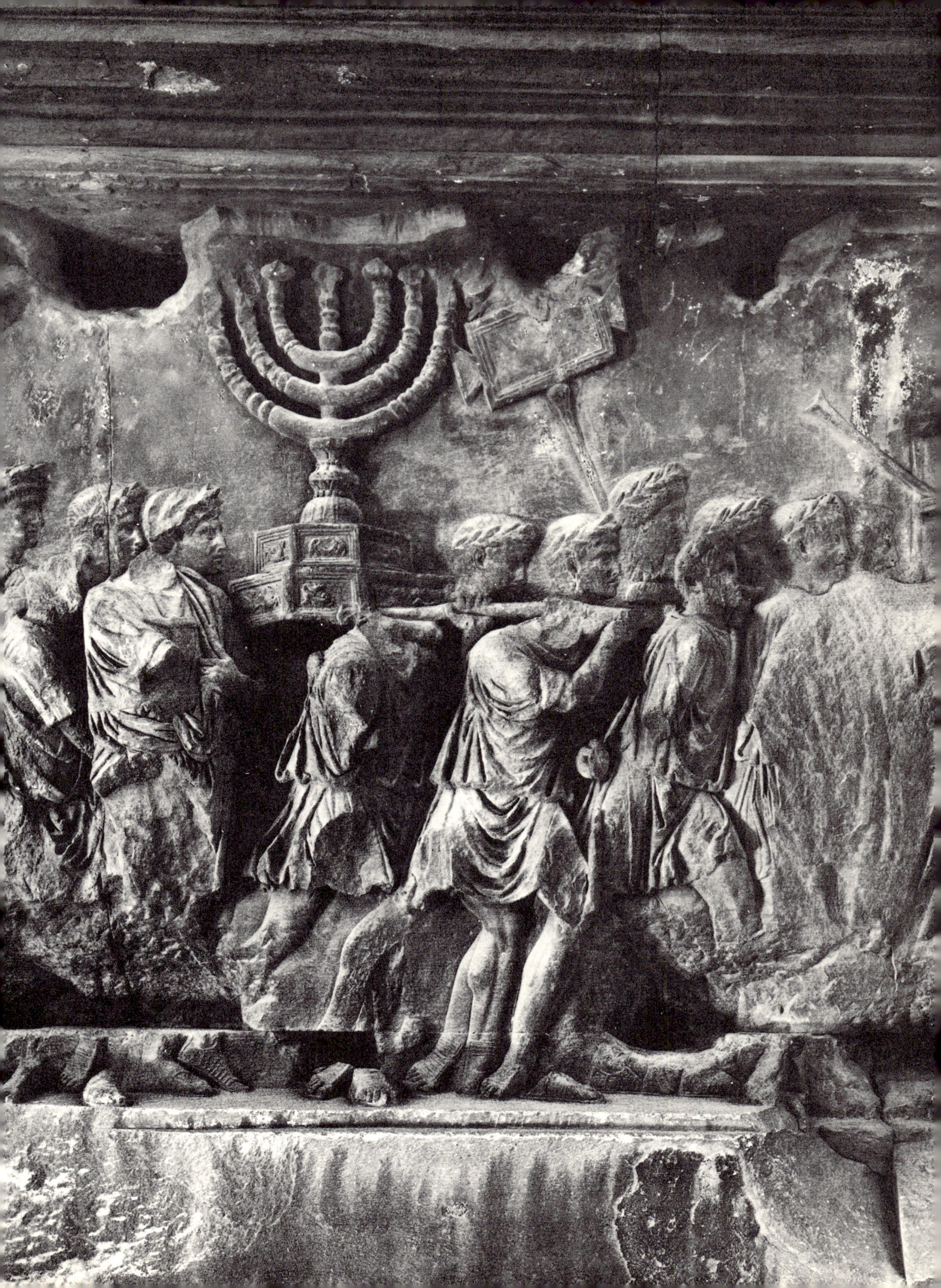

Vespasian

Titus *Domitian*

The Flavian Dynasty

The triumphal procession ended at the temple of Jupiter Capitolinus. It was the time-honored custom to wait there until the execution of the enemy's general was announced. This was Simon, son of Gioras, who had just taken part in the pageant among the prisoners. Now with a rope around him and scourged by his conductors, he was dragged to the usual spot in the Forum, where Roman law requires that malefactors condemned to death be executed. When the announcement was made that Simon was dead, shouts of applause greeted it. The princes then began the sacrifices, which having duly been offered with the customary prayers, they withdrew into the palace. Rome kept festival all that day for her victory in the campaign.

V

Meanwhile, Lucillus Bassus had been sent to Judea to take over command. He captured the fortress of Herodium, the burial place of King Herod. Then he moved his forces against the stronghold of Machaerus, which surrendered. Machaerus was a rocky hill, rising to an immense height and surrounded on all sides by deep ravines. About this time Vespasian sent instructions to Bassus to farm out all of the Jewish territory. Vespasian had not founded any settlements on the land, but had reserved it all as his personal property, with the exception of some small allotments granted to eight hundred discharged veterans of the wars. On all Jews he imposed a tax of two drachmae to be paid annually into the Capitol as formerly it had been paid to the Temple at Jerusalem. Such was the state of Jewish affairs at this time.

Lucillus Bassus died and was succeeded by Flavius Silva. All of Judea was now subjugated by Roman arms, with the ex-

OVERLEAF:
View of Masada from the north. The Romans reached the top by building the sloping embankment on the western side (right).
JEWISH MUSEUM. YIGAEL YADIN

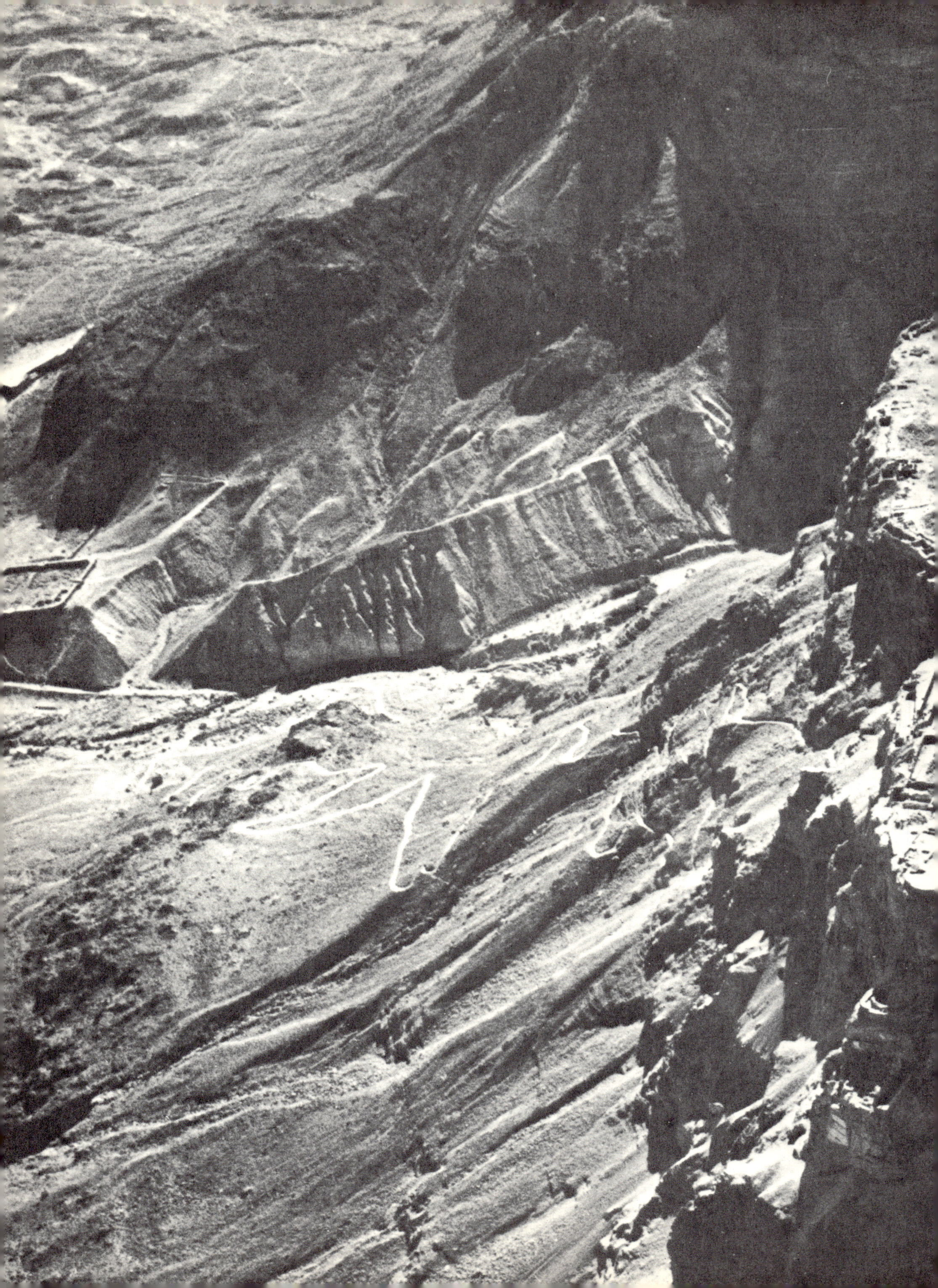

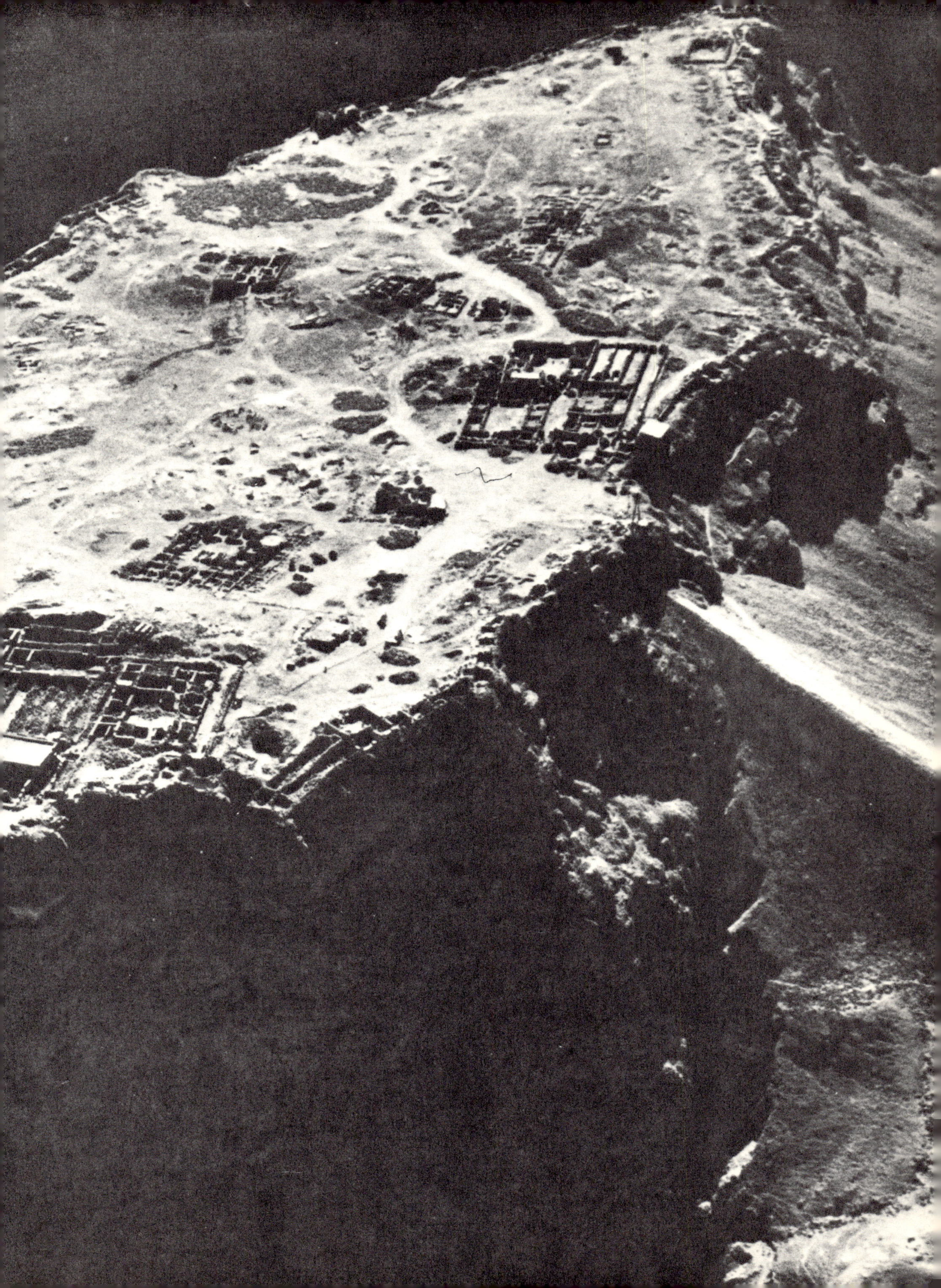

View of Masada from the south. The large rectangle in the valley is the remains of the Roman camp.
FOTOTECA UNIONE

73 A.D.

ception of one fortress, called Masada. The Zealots who occupied Masada were led by a descendant of one of the original leaders of the sect, who years earlier had urged the Jews to resist the Romans. The Zealot commander was called Eleazar, son of Yair.

Flavius Silva assembled all his forces and marched to attack Masada. The Roman general promptly made himself master of the whole district around the fortress and set up garrisons at the most strategic points. He threw up a wall all around to make it difficult for any of the besieged to escape and posted sentinels to guard it. He himself encamped at a spot where the fortress abutted on an adjacent mountain. The site was difficult to supply properly for not only did food have to be carried from a distance, at the cost of hard labor by the Jews conscripted for this duty, but even drinking water had to be brought in from afar. With his preliminary arrangements completed, Silva turned now to the siege, which demanded great skill and enormous effort because of the strength of the fortress.

Masada was on a rock of no small size, lofty from end to

end, and terminating on every side in deep ravines. It was inaccessible except in two places where the rock permits a difficult ascent. One of these paths led from the Dead Sea on the east, the other, an easier approach, came in from the west. The eastern path is called the Snake Path, because it resembles a reptile. Narrow and continually winding, the path was at the very edge of jutting cliffs and crags, frequently turning upon itself like a snake. It was a perilous climb, with yawning chasms on either side, winding three and a half miles in length to reach a summit, which was not a sharp peak but a level, expanding plain.

On this plateau, the High Priest Jonathan, brother of Judas Maccabaeus, had first erected a fortress and named it Masada. In later times the fortifications were undertaken with serious attention by King Herod. At first he enclosed the entire summit, which measured three-fourths of a mile, with a wall of white stone, eighteen feet high and twelve feet wide. On it stood thirty-seven towers, seventy-five feet high, from which access was provided to apartments constructed around the whole inside of the wall. The top itself was rich soil and was devoted to cultivation. There, too, Herod built a palace on the western slope, beneath the walls which protected the crest, and facing north. The palace wall was strong and of great height. It had four towers, ninety feet high. The interior of the palace—its living quarters, colonnades, and baths—was richly furnished, with much variety. At every spot used for living purposes, both on the summit and around the palace, Herod had cut out in the rock numerous large cisterns as reservoirs for water, thus

OVERLEAF:
The remains of Herod's palace on Masada.
MASADA EXPEDITION. YIGAEL YADIN

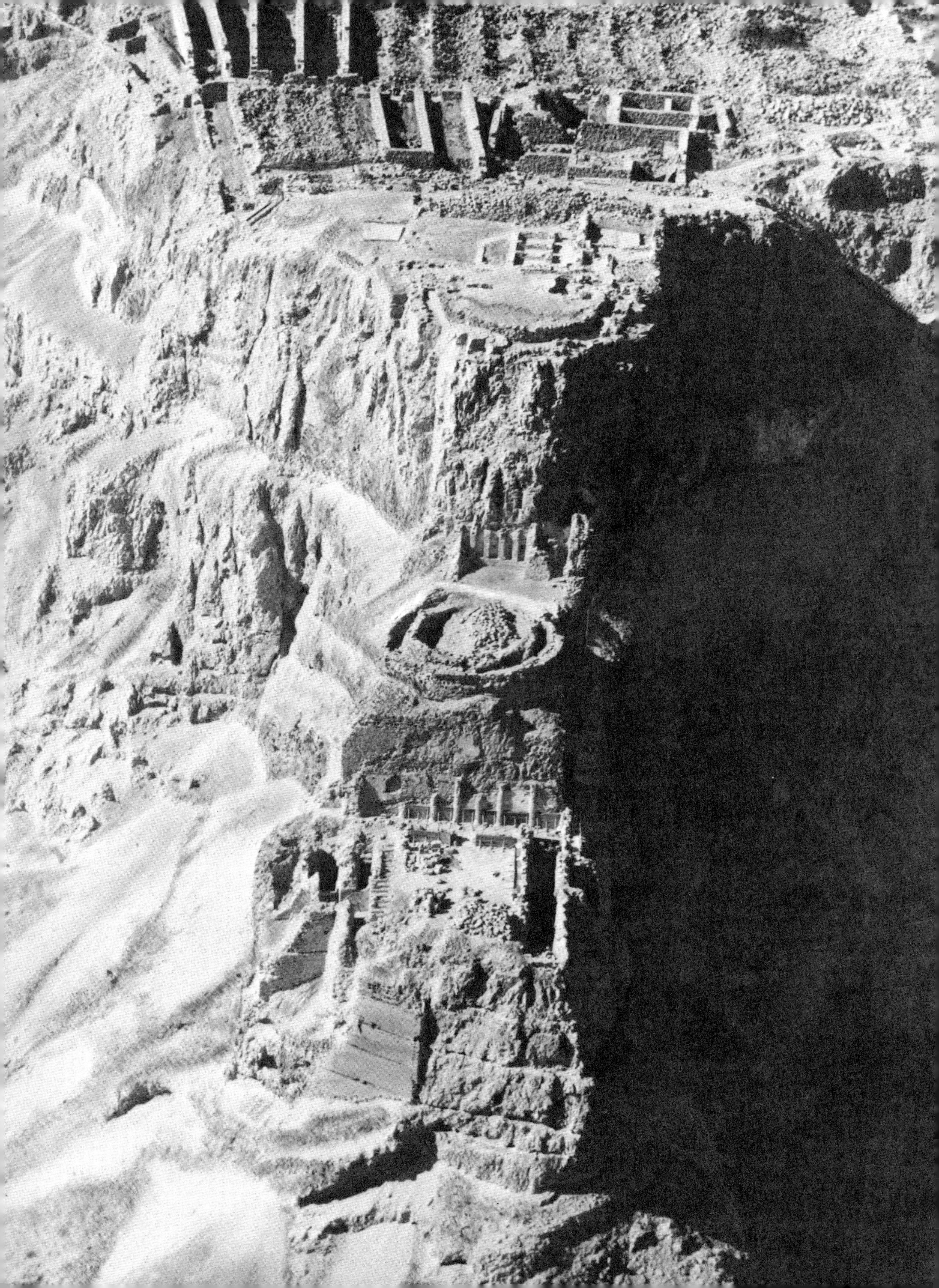

Lower terrace of Herod's palace with Corinthian columns.
JEWISH MUSEUM. ELIOT ELISOFON

making it possible to put in an ample supply. A hidden road led up from the palace to the summit, which could not be seen from the outside.

In addition, the stores inside the fortress were amazing because of their lavishness and splendor as well as for their state of preservation. For here had been stored a huge supply of corn, amply sufficient to last for years, abundance of wine and oil, besides every variety of seeds and piles of dates. These were found in perfect condition, as fresh and as good as the day they were first put in a hundred years earlier. It would not be incorrect to attribute the preservation to the high altitude of the plateau. There was also an abundance of arms of every description, stored there by Herod and sufficient for ten thousand men. Besides these there was a mass of unworked iron, brass, and lead. It is said that Herod outfitted this fortress as a refuge for himself, suspecting two dangers: one from the Jewish people who might depose him; and the second, greater and more serious, from Cleopatra, Queen of Egypt. She never hid her desire for the throne of Judea and constantly pleaded with Antony to slay Herod and give it to her. It was such fears that drove Herod to fortify Masada, which he left to the Romans as the final task in their war with the Jews.

Silva now completed his wall surrounding Masada and took every precaution that none should escape from it. He discovered only one spot where it was possible to construct earthworks. On the west face of the fortress, there was a projection of rock of considerable size, jutting far out, but still 450 feet below the summit. It was called the White Cliff. The Roman general climbed up and occupied this jutting ridge. He ordered his troops to throw up an earthen embankment, a solid bank, which they raised to the height of three hundred feet. But it was still not solid enough or big enough to hold the war engines. So on top of it was constructed a platform of great stones fitted closely together, seventy-five feet wide and just as long. The engines of war in general were similar to those built by Vespasian and Titus for their siege operations. In addition, a tower ninety feet high was constructed, entirely shielded by iron. On this the Romans mounted a number of quick-firers and stone-throwers with which they quickly beat off the defenders from the battlements and forced them to seek cover.

Simultaneously, Silva ordered his great battering ram to

start pounding the wall constantly, incessantly without relief. With difficulty, he succeeded in effecting a breach and brought the wall, which guarded the summit, down in ruins. The defenders, however, had already hastily built up another wall inside. This was not likely to meet with a similar fate from the Roman engines for it was pliable, designed to break the force of the battering blows. It was built of great wooden beams, laid lengthwise and end to end in two parallel rows a wall's breadth apart, with the space between filled with earth. The work presented the appearance of masonry, but the blows of the engines had little effect, since they were falling upon a yielding material. Observing this, Silva ordered his soldiers to destroy this inner wall by fire. Since it was made mainly of wood, it quickly caught fire, blazing up in flames. At first, a north wind blew back the flames, driving them against the Romans. The fear that all of their war engines would be burned up almost reduced the Romans to despair. But suddenly, as if by divine providence, the wind veered to the south. It blew with full force in the opposite direction and flung the flames against the defenders' wall, which was soon totally ablaze. The Romans returned to their camp rejoicing, determined to renew the attack on the following day. Throughout the night, they kept stricter watch lest any of the defenders escape.

However, Eleazar was not thinking of flight for himself, nor did he consider it for any one else. Seeing the wall going up in flames, left without any further means of resistance, he deliberated the fate before him and his followers. Thinking of the children and wives and of the terrible things they could expect from the victorious Romans, he assembled the bravest of his comrades and addressed them thus:

"Long ago, my brave men, we resolved neither to serve the Romans nor any other except our God. For He alone is man's true and righteous Lord. Now the time has come when we must test our resolution by our actions. At this crisis, let us not disgrace ourselves. We refused to submit to a slavery even when it meant no physical danger to us. Let us not now accept slavery, with all of the punishments awaiting us if we fall alive into Roman hands. For as we were the first of all to revolt, so are we the last in arms against them. Moreover, I believe that it is God who has granted us this favor, that we have it in our power to die nobly and in freedom, a privilege denied to others who were met with unexpected defeat.

"Our fate at break of day is certain capture. But there is still the free choice of a noble death in the company of those we hold most dear. Our enemies cannot prevent this even though they fervently hope to take us alive. Nor can we hope to defeat them in battle. Maybe, indeed, from the very first—when we chose to defend our liberty—we ought perhaps to have read God's purpose and to have recognized that the Jewish people, once beloved by Him, had been sentenced to extinction. For had He continued to be gracious, or even just a little angry, He would never have permitted such widespread destruction or have abandoned His most Holy City to be burned to the ground by our enemies. But did we, in truth, really hope that we alone of all the Jewish nation would survive and preserve our freedom? Mark now how He exposes the vanity of our hopes. Not even

A coin of the revolt inscribed "Shekel of Israel Year 3."

The reverse displays three pomegranates. The inscription reads "Jerusalem the Holy."
FOTOTECA UNIONE

the impregnable nature of this fortress has been enough to save us. Nay, though we have ample food, stores of arms, plenty for every other need, yet we have been deprived, manifestly by God Himself, of all hope of surviving. For it was not of their own accord that those flames which were driving against the enemy turned back upon the wall which we built. No, all this betokens God's wrath.

"But let us not pay the penalty for our sins to our bitterest foes, the Romans, but rather to God Himself, through an act of our own hands. Let our wives die undishonored, our children with no knowledge of slavery. And when they are gone, let us render ungrudging service to each other, using our liberty as a noble winding sheet. But first let us destroy our possessions and the whole fortress by fire, for the Romans will be deeply chagrined to find neither our persons nor anything of value to loot. Let us spare only our food supply, for it will testify, when we are dead, that it was not want which subdued us, but that, as we resolved at the beginning of the war, we chose death, not slavery."

Thus spoke Eleazar, but his words did not touch the hearts of all hearers alike. Some were eager to do as he said, finding themselves filled with delight at the thought of a death so noble. But others, less heroic, were moved by pity for their wives and families. Eleazar, seeing that many of his people were flinching from his plan, was afraid that even those who had heard him with courage might be weakened by the tears and sighs of the faint-hearted. Fired with a mighty fervor, he roused himself to a higher flight of oratory.

"Consider all those Jews in our own land who went to war with Rome," he cried passionately. "They had everything that could fire them with hopes of victory! Arms, battlements, impregnable fortresses, and a spirit afraid of no dangers in the cause of liberty. Yet these were effective but for a brief season. After buoying us with hopes, they proved only the beginnings of greater disasters. Those men who fell in battle may be deemed lucky for they died defending liberty, not betraying it.

"But the multitudes now in Roman hands, who would not pity? Who would not rush to die rather than share their fate? Of them, some have perished on the rack, or been tortured to death by fire or by the lash. Others, half-devoured by wild beasts, have been rescued alive to be a second repast for the animals, just to provide amusement and sport for their foes. Most miserable of all are those still alive. How often have they prayed for death but it never comes!"

Eleazar then mourned for the whole Jewish race and for Jerusalem.

"Where now is that great city, the mother city of the Jews, entrenched behind so many walls, sheltered behind so many forts and towers, defended by so many thousands of heroic men? What has become of her that was believed to have God for a founder? She has been torn up by the roots and swept away. Her sole memorial are the dead still buried in her ruins. Only miserable old men sit beside the ashes of the shrine. Which of us, knowing this, could bear to behold the sun, even if he could live safely, free from peril? Who hates his country so much, who is so unmanly, so fond of life, that he is not sorry to be alive today? I wish that we had all died before we saw the Holy City razed by an enemy's hands, and the Holy Sanctuary so profanely destroyed.

"We have been misled by an honorable hope that we might succeed in avenging her, but now that hope has vanished. So let us hasten to die honorably. Let us have pity on ourselves, our children, and our wives, while we can. For we were born for death, we and those whom we have begotten. But outrage and slavery and the sight of our wives being led to shame with their children—these are not necessary evils imposed by nature

During Roman victory celebrations, thousands of Jewish prisoners died in battles against wild beasts.

A pottery sherd found on Masada, inscribed with the name "Ben Ya'ir"—perhaps a lottery token.
MASADA EXPEDITION. YIGAEL YADIN

on mankind. They come about through the cowardice of those who, having the chance of forestalling them by death, refuse to take it. We are very proud of our courage. So we revolted from Rome. Now at the end, they have offered to spare our lives. But we have spurned them. Is anyone so blind that he will not see how furious they will be when they take us alive?

"Pity the young, whose vigorous bodies can sustain prolonged tortures, pity the more advanced in years too weak to bear such calamities. Is a man to see his wife led off to violation, to hear the voice of his child crying 'Father,' when his own hands are bound? No, while those hands are free and can hold a sword, let us die as free men with our children and wives. Let us quit this life together!"

Eleazar would have continued his plea but he was cut short by his hearers who were now overpowered by an uncontrollable impulse to accomplish the deed at once. Like men possessed, they rushed to outdo one another, as though it were a sign of courage and judgment not to be among the last to stay alive. They took their wives and children in their arms, clinging to them with tears and with parting kisses and caresses. At that instant, as though guided by other hands than their own, they performed their purpose. All carried the task through with their dearest ones. What wretched victims of fate, to whom the slaying with their own hands of their wives and children seemed so slight an evil. Then unable to endure their grief, they quickly piled up all the stores in the fortress and set them on fire. They then chose by lot ten of their number to dispatch all the rest and so laid themselves down, each beside his fallen wife and children. Enfolding their dear ones in their arms, they offered their own throats to the sword. The chosen ten, having slaughtered all, set up the same rule of chance for each other, that the one chosen by lot would slay first the nine remaining and then himself. The nine bared their throats, and the last solitary survivor, after surveying the prostrate multitude, set the palace ablaze. Collecting his strength, he drove his sword clean through his own body and fell dead beside his family.

The Zealots had died in the belief that they had not left a soul alive to fall into Roman hands. But an old woman and a relative of Eleazar escaped with five children. They concealed themselves in an underground reservoir, while the rest were absorbed in the heroic suicide. The victims numbered 960, including women and children.

May 2, 73 A.D.

The Romans, expecting further resistance, were under arms at daybreak and advanced to the assault. Not a single defender was to be seen. On all sides there was an awesome silence. They were at a loss to guess what had happened. At last they called out to any one within. Their shouts were heard by the old women, who emerged from the caverns and informed the Romans of the deed and how it was done. When they came upon the rows upon rows of the dead, the Roman enemies admired the nobility and utter contempt for death displayed by so many.

Masada being thus taken, the Roman general left a garrison on the spot and he departed. For not an enemy of Rome remained throughout the country, the whole having now been subdued by this protracted war.

To remind Rome of the Judean conquest, coins portrayed a sorrowing Jewess guarded by a Roman, with the legend "Judea Capta"—Judea is fallen.
AMERICAN NUMISMATIC SOCIETY

Here we close the history, which we promised to relate with perfect accuracy for the information of those who wish to learn how this war was waged by the Romans against the Jews. Of the style of this history I leave my readers to judge. But as to its truth, I say that, throughout the entire account, it has been my single aim.

INDEX

Acrabetta, 48, 82
Adida, 79
Agrippa I, 24, 103
Agrippa II, Marcus Julius, 38–42, 45, 50, 51, 55, 66, 68, 80
Albinus, 37
Alexander the Great, 13–14
Alexander, Tiberius, 85, 90
Alexandra, 16–17
Alexandria, 45, 55, 85, 86, 89, 109, 131
Ananus, 48, 76, 77
Antioch, 13, 45, 55, 86
Antiochus IV, 15, 16, 45, 129
Antipater, 17, 19
Antipater (son of Herod), 20
Antony, Mark, 19, 20, 146
Archelaus, 20, 21
Arch of Titus, 29
Aristobulos, 17–18
Asochaeus, 129

Babylon, 13, 14, 122, 124
Bassus, Lucillus, 139
Berenice, 24, 39, 40, 50
Bersabe, 48

Caesar, Augustus, 12, 19, 117

Caesarea, 19, 36–37, 38, 39, 43, 45, 64, 66, 79, 80, 82, 84, 86, 90, 130
Caesarea-Philippi, 21, 66, 130
Caesar, Julius, 12, 19
Caligula, Gaius, 23–24
Canaan, 129
Claudius, 24–25, 55
Cleopatra, 19–20, 146
Cumanus, 25
"curved daggers" (see Sicarri)
Cyrus the Great, 13, 124

David, King, 14, 103, 129
Dead Sea, 7, 79, 143
Domitian, 86, 131, 134

Edom (see Idumaea)
Egypt, 13, 14, 19–20, 85, 90, 128, 131
Eleazar, 36
Eleazar, son of Simon, 48, 89, 100, 106
Eleazar, son of Yair, 43, 142, 147–152, 153
Essenes, 17

Felix, Marcus Antonius, 25–26, 36, 37
Festus, 37
Florus, Gessius, 37–41, 46, 48

157

Gadara, 78
Galba, 80
Galilee, 13, 16, 19, 21–22, 45, 48–49, 56, 57
  campaign of, 8, 67–75
  Sea of, 21, 24, 51, 66, 68, 71
Gallus, Cestius, 37, 39–40, 45–48, 90
Gamala, 48, 71–73
Gaul, 79, 80, 131
Gerasa, 79
Gibeon, 45, 47
Gischala, 49, 71–75
Gophna, 48, 82, 99
Greece, culture of, 14

Hanukkah, festival of, 15
Hasmonean family, 15
Hebron, 81, 82
Herod Antipas, 20–23, 103
Herod the Great, King, 17, 19–20, 37, 103, 129, 143, 145–146
Herodium, 82, 139
Hyrcanus, John, 16
Hyrcanus, 17–18, 19, 20 (tomb of), 106

Idumaea (*Edom*), 13, 16, 48, 77, 79, 81–82, 83, 105
Israel, 14

Jannaeus, Alexander, 16
Japhna, 48
Jericho, 48, 78, 79
Jerusalem, 8, 11, 13, 14, 15, 17–18, 19, 23, 24, 25, 29, 36, 37, 51, 52, 65, 79–80, 81, 82, 83, 84, 89, 105, 118, 127–28, 129–30, 131, 148, 150–151
  Acra (the Citadel), 101
  history of (prior to Roman era), 13, 129
  internal strife, 75–78, 83–84, 89, 100–101, 106, 117
  Lower City, 90, 101, 127
  palace of king, 103–104, 127
  Serpents' Pool, 101
  siege of, 8, 99–129
  starvation, 110, 114, 115, 117
  Stronghold of King David, 101
  Temple (enclosure), 19, 20, 24, 38, 39, 41–42, 46, 76, 83, 89–90, 99, 100–101, 103, 104, 105–106, 112, 117, 119, 120, 121, 129–31
    Antonia (fortress), 20, 39, 41, 42, 115, 117, 118–20, 121
    towers of, 101, 103
  Temple, Holy, 8, 11, 15, 18, 20, 24, 41, 104, 121–24, 125–26, 134
    Altar, 90, 104, 123
    gates of, 89, 121–22, 126
    Holy of Holies, 105
    Holy Place, 76, 90, 104–5, 120, 123–24
    Sanctuary, 29, 76, 100–01, 104–05, 123, 151
  Upper Agora (Market), 101
  Upper City, 42, 90, 101, 112, 127–8
Jewish War, The, 12, 27, 29
Jews
  anti-Roman spirit, 25–26
  conquest tax on, 139
  massacres, 15, 25, 38, 43, 45, 47, 62, 68, 77, 79, 82, 124, 128
  religious sensibilities of, 12–13, 15, 16, 23, 29
  toll among Jews, 128
John of Gischala, 49–51, 73, 75, 76–77, 78, 80–81, 83–84, 89–90, 100–01, 105–06, 114, 117, 118, 119–20, 126–27, 128, 131
John, son of Levi (*see* John of Gischala)
Jonathan, 143
Joppa, 64
Jordan River, 79
Joseph, son of Gorion, 48
Josephus, Flavius (*Matthias, Joseph ben*), 7, 8, 12, 19, 23, 24, 27, 29, 30, 35–36
  commander in Galilee, 35, 48–51, 56, 57–58, 60–63
  prisoner of Romans, 35, 64, 85, 112, 114, 120, 127

Jotapata, 48, 58–62, 64, 71
Judah of Galilee, 20–21
Judea, 11, 13, 14, 15–16, 17–19, 20, 21, 23, 24–26, 37, 39, 55, 79, 80, 82, 86, 90, 139, 142

Maccabaeus, Judas, 15, 16, 143
Macedon, 13
Machaerus, 82, 139
Mariamme, 20, 41
Masada, 11, 20, 27, 29, 41, 42, 43, 52, 78, 80, 82, 142, 143
    archeological story of, 7, 29–30
    siege of, 7, 8, 23, 142–53
    Snake Path, the, 143
    White Cliff, 146
    palace of Herod, 8, 20, 143
    plea of Eleazar, son of Yair, 148–52
Melchi-Zedek, 129
Menahem, 42-43

Neapolitanus, 39–40
Nebuchadnezzar, 13, 122, 129
Nero, 23, 36–38, 48, 55, 64, 68, 80, 85
Nicanor, 62

Olives, Mount of, 99
Otho, 80, 82

Palestine, 13
Peraea, 48, 78–79
Persia, 13
Pharisees, 17
Philip, 20–21
Phoenicia, 13, 64
Pilate, Pontius, 23
Pompey the Great, 18–19, 129
Ptolemies, rule of, in Egypt, 13

Rome, the city, 55, 86, 131
    internal strife, 84
    triumphal procession in, 128, 131, 134
Rome, the Empire, 11, 14, 17–18, 21, 85
    internal troubles, 18–19, 79, 80
    effect of Judean war on, 12
    tax levied on Jews, 139

Sadducees, 17
Samaria, 13, 99
Scopus (*Lookout Hill*), 46, 99, 101
Seleucids, 13, 14, 16
Sepphoris, 56
Sicarii ("curved daggers"), 36, 78
Silva, Flavius, 139, 142, 146–47
Simon, 15–16
Simon, son of Gioras, 52, 81–84, 90, 101, 103, 105, 114-5, 119–20, 126-7, 128-9, 131, 136
Solomon, King, 14, 103, 124
Syria, 13, 14, 15, 16, 18, 39, 45, 55, 64, 80, 130

Tabor, Mt., 71, 73
Tarichaeae, 48, 50, 66, 68, 71
Thamnia, 48
Tiberias, 48, 51, 58, 66, 68, 71
Tiberius, 24
Titus, 8, 55, 56, 64, 66–68, 73, 75, 80, 86, 89, 90, 106, 130, 131, 134, 146

Valley of Thorns, 99
Vespasian, 8, 12, 55, 77–80, 82, 84–86, 90, 99, 124, 129, 131, 134, 139, 146
Vitellius, 80, 82, 84, 85, 86

Zealots, 7, 8, 23, 30, 42, 76, 77, 78, 81, 82, 83–84, 89, 101, 106, 118, 120, 142, 153